THE COMPLETE GUIDE TO
HOME MOSAICS

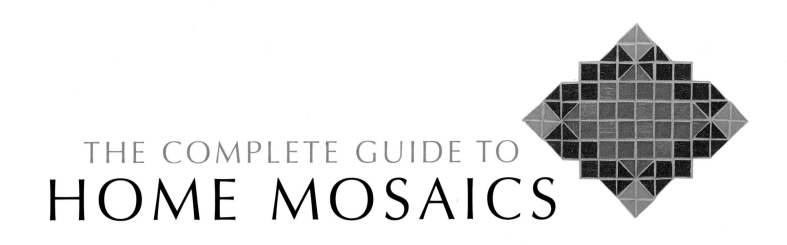

Select Editions, Vancouver

THE COMPLETE GUIDE TO
HOME MOSAICS

LIVING ROOM & DINING ROOM PROJECTS

KITCHEN & BATHROOM PROJECTS

CONTENTS

INTRODUCING MOSAICS

Mosaic design has often been described as "painting by numbers," and however basic a description this might be, it does provide a clue to this art form's key attraction—its accessibility. Mosaics are simply the creation of patterns and pictures from pieces of stone, ceramic, porcelain, or glass … what could be simpler?

Mosaic designs range from very simple to very detailed—both can be beautiful. Start with straightforward designs, and as you gain confidence, move on to more ambitious projects. Experiment with different materials and patterns.

You will soon discover why mosaics have existed as an art form for over 2000 years— some of the earliest examples of mosaics are from ancient Mesopotamia, and are believed to date back to around 3000 B.C. Their combination of decorative and functional attributes have ensured that this versatile and durable art form has a timeless appeal. All you need to enjoy mosaic design is time, patience, and imagination.

MATERIALS

Tesserae (which comes from the Latin word for "square" and the Greek word for "four") is the name of the pieces used to make mosaics. They come in all shapes and sizes, and are supplied loose or on sheets. When storing tesserae, you need to make them easily identifiable, so glass or transparent containers are ideal for loose cubes, and clearly labeled boxes work well for flat sheets. All adhesives, cements, and additives are best stored in a dry, cool place.

Below is a list of the main materials used in mosaic design. However, there are no rules, and mosaicists can use any number of other materials, including glass beads, buttons, coins, shells, slate, semiprecious stones, and broken household china.

Marble Available in a natural palette of colors, marble tesserae have either polished or unpolished finishes: the former gives a smooth, elegant look, whereas the latter has a more rustic appeal. Cut marble using a hammer and hardy (see page 8) and protect with a sealant. Commonly used pieces are ⅝ x ⅝in (1.5 x 1.5cm).

Vitreous glass Available in many colors, these are relatively cheap and resistant to heat and frost, making them ideal for both interior and exterior use. Cut glass using mosaic nippers (see page 8). They are usually supplied in single-color sheets of ¾ x ¾in (2 x 2cm), or loose in bags of mixed colors.

Porcelain These are usually supplied unglazed and are available in numerous colors. Suited to both internal and external application, they have excellent slip-resistant properties even when wet. Use mosaic nippers to cut them (see page 8) and seek advice from your tile supplier regarding sealants.

Ceramic These are similar to porcelain tesserae except that they are usually glazed.

Smalti These are made from glass, which is prepared and cut into rectangular strips and then into rectangular tesserae. The irregularities of the hand-cut glass surfaces reflect light beautifully. Sold in 1lb (500g) or 2lb (1kg) bags, usually in ½ x ⅝in (1 x 1.5cm) pieces, smalti are relatively expensive but worth every cent. They can be used internally and externally because they are resistant to heat and frost. Use a hammer and hardy to cut them (see page 8).

Gold or silver leaf To make these tesserae, a thin layer of 24-carat gold or silver is hammered onto a colored glass backing and covered with a veneer of glass. This is then hand cut into tesserae, which can lead to irregularities in size and shape. They are available with either a flat or rippled surface. Use them for decorative purposes only, because the silver or gold breaks down in conditions such as extreme heat and frost.

Pebbles and stones These are available in a variety of colors, sizes, and textures. Granite and other hard stones are recommended for their durability, and they can be used internally and externally.

Household ceramic tiles These come in many colors and sizes. They are inexpensive, which makes experimental cutting affordable. Always check the durability of the tiles, because certain types are prone to cracking under extreme conditions.

Glass and mirror Use these to add a reflective quality to your mosaics. They are available in large panels from glass and some tile suppliers, and should be cut very carefully with glass cutters.

BASIC TOOLS & TECHNIQUES

The basic mosaic tool kit is very simple, and you may already have some of this equipment around your home. If not, visit a hardware store, builder's supplier, or tile supplier (see page 112).

1. Hardy This is used with a hammer for cutting marble and smalti. The hardy is a small metal block with a chisel-type blade, which can either be embedded in concrete in a flowerpot or in an upright log.

2. Hammer This is curved on one edge and tipped with tungsten carbide for durability. There are various weights of hammer—choose one that feels comfortable to you and is in proportion with the hardy.

3. Mouth and nose filter mask Wear this when cutting tesserae, mixing grout and cement, or using strong-smelling solvents.

4. Mosaic nippers These are used to cut vitreous glass, porcelain, and ceramic tesserae. The cutting edge is usually tipped with tungsten carbide for durability. Buy nippers with spring-action handles to make cutting less arduous.

5. Tile cutters These cutters carve through tiles in a two-step process. One part of the cutters has a small wheel or blade; the other part has a flat edge known as the snapper. First, the tile is scored with the blade; then, it is "snapped" with the flat edge.

6. Electric drill This is used for attaching mosaic projects to walls or other surfaces. Buy a selection of plastic wall anchors and screws, and invest in a countersink bit, which hides screwheads. A jigsaw is also a useful tool for delicate, intricate cutting.

7. Gummed brown paper When dampened, the gum bonds tesserae temporarily, which is ideal for the indirect method (see page 11). You can also use plain brown paper, but you will need to apply gum glue to the matte side.

8. Wood Used as a base material or support, the type of wood you use will depend on the weight and size of your mosaic project, and whether it will be used inside or outside. Always prime before use.

9. Paintbrush/glue spreader These are used to paint/prime surfaces and apply glue.

10. Polyvinyl acetate (PVA) glue This is excellent for priming or preparing surfaces.

11. Tape measure/ruler Measuring tools.

12. Level This has a liquid measure with a bubble in it. When the bubble is central in the liquid, the surface being measured is straight.

13. Safety glasses Wear these when cutting tesserae, as slivers can damage your eyes.

14. Scissors Cutting tool for paper/card.

15. Gum glue This is a water-based adhesive. It is applied to plain brown paper when using the indirect method (see page 11).

16. Tweezers These are wonderful for picking up small tesserae and positioning them, or for removing unwanted pieces.

17. Awl This makes an excellent "pricking-out" implement for removing unwanted cement and mosaics.

18. Craft knife Cutting tool for paper/card.

19. String Useful for creating large circles.

20. Masking tape This is not as sticky as adhesive tape, so it is ideal for attaching templates to tracing paper temporarily.

21. Graph and sketch paper These are especially useful during the design stages.

22. Markers, pens, and pencils Use markers to draw your design on the base material. Pens and pencils are essential throughout.

SAFETY ADVICE

When cutting
▸ wear surgical gloves, safety glasses, and a mouth and nose filter mask
▸ wear close-toed shoes
▸ lay drop cloths if working inside

When applying adhesives, grouts, and sealants
▸ follow manufacturers' instructions
▸ wear surgical or rubber gloves
▸ work in well-ventilated areas; use a filter mask if necessary
▸ wear an apron or smock
▸ lay drop cloths

When drilling
▸ always unplug when changing bits
▸ wear safety glasses

CUTTING & SCORING

MOSAIC NIPPERS: These are used to cut vitreous glass and porcelain tesserae. Hold the nippers in one hand and the tessera in the other. Before cutting, get used to handling the nippers, which should be held toward the bottom of the handles. Place the tessera face up between the cutting edges of the nippers and then apply firm pressure.

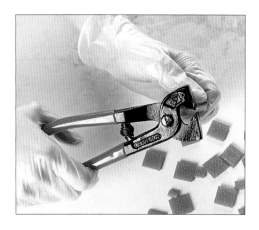

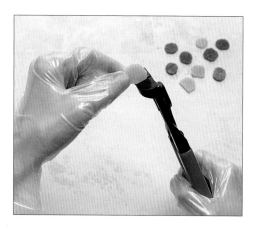

Cutting in half Place the tessera halfway into the mosaic nippers. Squeeze the handles firmly and the tessera will break in half. If you need quarters, repeat the procedure with half a tessera. The quarters can also be cut in half to create smaller tesserae that are ideal for outlining.

Cutting diagonals Place the tessera diagonally between the cutting edges of the nippers. Apply pressure and the piece should break into two triangles.

Cutting curves or circles This shape is slightly more difficult to perfect than halves or diagonals, but can be achieved if you nip off each corner of the tessera. Then, slowly "nibble" all the way around the tile to produce a smooth circular or oval shape.

HAMMER AND HARDY: Used to cut smalti and marble, this is similar to a tool used by the Romans. Make sure that your cutting hand is not restricted while you work and be patient—perfect results take time.

TILE CUTTERS: These are useful if you want to cut ceramic tiles that measure more than 1in (2.5cm) square, and are ideal if you are using spare tiles left over from the bathroom or kitchen. The cutters have a dual function: first, the blade scores a line along the tile; then, the snappers break it. For ceramic squares, cut strips and then score and snap them into squares. You can get larger cutters or cutting machines for cutting thicker, tougher tiles.

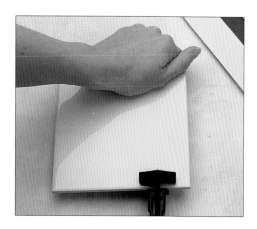

Hammer and hardy Position the tessera over the blade of the hardy where you want the cut to be. Bring the hammer down lightly and firmly on the center of the tessera. Avoid inhaling dust by not cutting directly under your nose.

Scoring tiles To produce a scored line on a ceramic tile, place a metal ruler in the exact position that you want the cutting line to be. Then run the tile cutters' blade along the edge of the metal ruler, applying even pressure as you go.

Snapping tiles Put the tile cutters' "snappers" over the center of the scored line. Use your other hand to take the pressure away from the cut. Apply firm pressure to the cutters until you hear a snapping noise when the tile is cut.

ADHESIVES, GROUTS, & TOOLS

There are different types of adhesives and grouts available and it is important that you choose the correct one for your project's requirements.

1. Polyvinyl acetate (PVA) glue (illustrated on page 7) A white glue available in two forms: water soluble and non-water soluble. The former can be used in the direct method (see page 10). Also used to prime surfaces.

2. Gum glue (illustrated on page 7) This is usually water soluble and is used for the indirect method (see page 11).

3. Cement-based adhesive This is available in powder, ready-mixed, or rapid-setting forms. Using an additive will allow more movement and flexibility.

4. Mortar (not illustrated) Made from sand, cement, and water, this is ideal for exterior floor mosaics. The ratio is generally 3:1 coarse sand to cement.

5. Grout Used to fill the gaps between the tesserae, this comes in ready-mixed or powder form and in a variety of colors. The cement-based powder form is illustrated here. Ready-made products are also available, but they tend to leave a residue behind.

6. Epoxy grout (not illustrated) This is a two-part, resin-based grout that creates a waterproof barrier.

7. Paint scraper This can be used to mix and apply small amounts of adhesive and grout.

8. Notched trowel Used for laying adhesive, the notched edge combs the adhesive to ensure an even layer and create a good tooth for the tiles to bond to. A ¼in (3mm) trowel is recommended because it creates a smaller grooved bed that is ideal for mosaics.

9. Trowel Use a pointed trowel for applying adhesive in small, awkward areas, and for measuring and mixing adhesive and grout.

10. Margin trowel Square-headed trowel.

11. Palette knives Available in different-shaped heads, this flexible tool is great for applying adhesive or grout in small areas, and for smoothing and removing excess.

12. Protective gloves Use rubber gloves when cleaning and grouting, and surgical gloves when applying adhesive and cutting tesserae.

13. Grout float or squeegee Used for applying grout, especially on large projects, and for removing grout residue.

14. Cloth Use for polishing grout residue.

15. Tiler's sponge Fine-grained sponge ideal for removing grout and cleaning. Use circular movements to ensure even coverage.

16. Sealant A wide variety of sealants are available—seek advice from a tile supplier for the product most suited to your project.

17. Additive for adhesive This is added to powder adhesive to allow greater movement. It is especially important when working on wood and floorboards.

18. Additive for grout This is used with powder grout to increase the grout's flexibility. Read the label for safety advice.

19. Measuring cups Used when measuring ratios of water, grout, and adhesive.

MIXING CEMENT AND GROUT

Measuring ingredients Follow the manufacturers' instructions with regard to quantities and ratios of ingredients—you can use various measuring devices, such as one full trowel or one full measuring cup to represent one unit of material.

Adding water Pour the ingredients into a clean bucket. Slowly add water and additive, and mix with a trowel.

Smoothing the mixture Using a small trowel, mix the ingredients thoroughly. The texture should be smooth and free from lumps, and neither too runny, nor too thick.

DIRECT MOSAIC-LAYING METHOD

 As the name suggests, this method involves applying the tesserae "directly" (face up) into position. This technique is useful because it enables you to see the final work progress piece by piece. It is used mostly in three-dimensional projects, on uneven surfaces, in mosaic murals, and backsplashes. It is not recommended for flat surfaces because the results may be irregular.

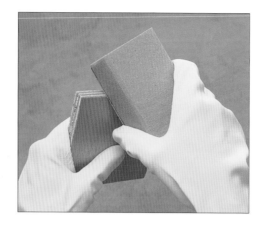

1 Run some sandpaper wrapped around a block of wood across the surface you are going to tile to provide a good tooth for the adhesive to bind to. Sand any rough edges.

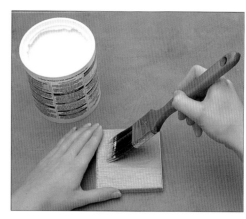

2 Paint the front and side edges with one coat of PVA glue to prime the surface. Make sure you clean your brush immediately after use or it will become stiff.

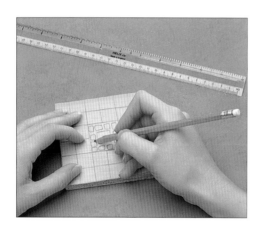

3 While you are waiting for the glue to dry, start to cut the mosaic pieces (see page 8) and prepare the adhesive. Once the glue has dried completely, draw your design on the primed surface with a pencil or marker pen.

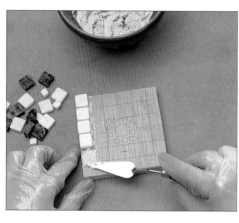

4 Spread the adhesive onto the base using a palette knife (or a notched trowel for large projects). Put the tesserae in place following the outline of the design. Allow the cement-based adhesive to dry for 24 hours.

5 Prick out excess cement with an awl or similar tool. If you leave it, it will be visible through the grout. Wash it away with a sponge and water. If using marble tesserae, apply a coat of marble protector.

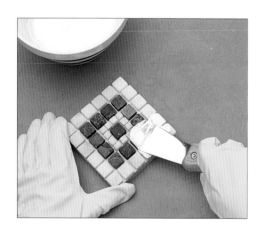

6 Put on rubber gloves and mix a quantity of grout (see page 9). Use a palette knife, squeegee, or paint scraper to squeeze the grout in the gaps between the tiles. Use a grout float for large projects.

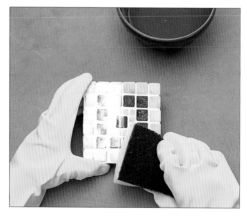

7 Using a clean, damp sponge, remove the excess grout. Repeat this process several times, and rinse the sponge regularly to keep it clean and avoid smearing.

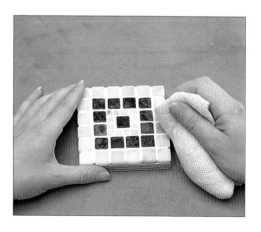

8 Use a cloth to polish the surface and remove any residue. Allow the grout to dry for 24 hours, then apply a sealant with a paintbrush or cloth. This is particularly important if the mosaic is made of marble.

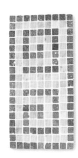

The indirect method involves laying the mosaics in reverse: draw the design back to front on gummed brown paper and stick the tesserae in position. When the mosaic is complete on paper, apply it to the permanent base in a bed of adhesive. Wash off the paper to reveal the design, then grout. Use this method for flat surfaces and large projects.

1 Draw your design. Trace onto tracing paper, turn the paper over, then transfer the design onto brown paper (sticky or matte side up) with the design in reverse.

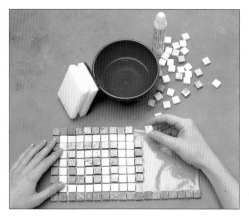

2 Stick the tesserae in position face down on the paper. For gummed paper, use water to bond the tesserae. For plain paper, use a water-soluble glue, such as gum glue.

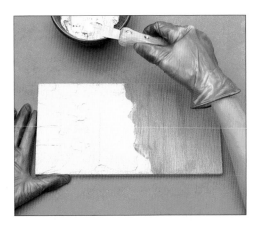

3 Prepare some cement-based adhesive using the method outlined on page 9. Apply to the surface using a paint scraper, or a trowel for large projects. Prime the surface before you begin, especially if using wood.

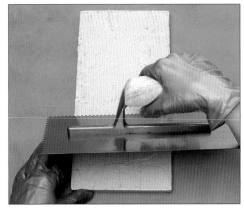

4 Drag a notched trowel at a 45° angle toward you in one sweeping action. This creates a grooved surface in the adhesive, which provides a good tooth into which the tesserae can bond.

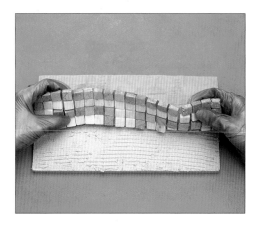

5 Carefully lift the mosaic and align its top edge with the top of the wood. Slowly lower the mosaic onto the adhesive. Smooth and press the tesserae with your hands. Allow to dry for 24 hours.

6 To reveal the design, moisten the paper with a wet sponge and then peel it off. Remove excess cement by "pricking" it out with an awl or similar tool. If using marble, apply a marble protector at this stage.

7 Wearing rubber gloves, prepare and apply grout, then remove any excess with a damp sponge. Rinse the sponge frequently or you will simply smear the grout instead of removing it. Allow to dry for 24 hours.

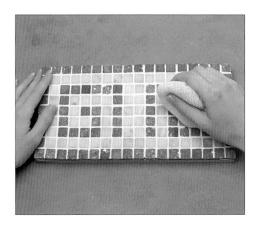

8 Polish the mosaic with a cloth to remove the fine layer of grout residue, then apply a sealant with a paintbrush or cloth. This is particularly important if the mosaic is made of marble.

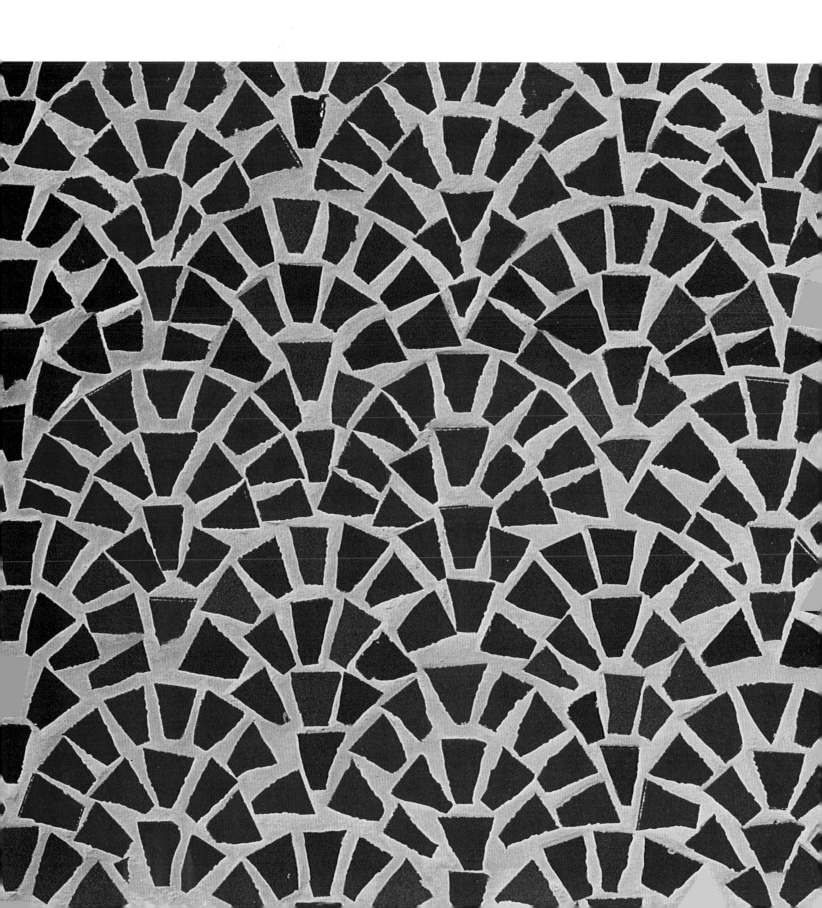

LIVING ROOMS & DINING ROOMS

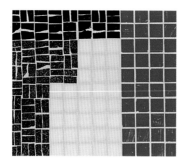

Japanese Sushi Table

TOOLS AND MATERIALS

Pencil
Ruler
Level
Sandpaper and block
Surgical and rubber gloves
Table: 35in (90cm) long
x 22in (55cm) wide
Vitreous glass tesserae:
¾ x ¾in (2 x 2cm)
Mosaic nippers
Safety glasses and mask
PVA glue and paintbrush
Gummed brown paper, or plain
brown paper and gum glue:
24in (60cm) long x 16in (40cm)
wide or the size of your table
Two buckets and a trowel
Awl or similar tool
Notched trowel: ¼in (3mm)
Sponge and cloth
Gray powder adhesive
and additive
White powder grout
and additive
Clear marine varnish
Black latex paint
Tracing paper

GLASS TESSERAE COLORS

Brown
Fire engine red
Pebble gray
Misty white
Shiny black
Charcoal

This beautiful, Japanese-inspired sushi table will look very stylish in any home. To create it, either use an existing table and reinvent it, or make a new one from scratch. The geometric pattern on the tabletop reflects a simple, abstract Zen style that creates an interesting focal point at meals and provides a perfect backdrop to the delights of the Japanese delicacy of sushi—dainty packages of seaweed, rice, and raw or cooked fish. The pattern consists mainly of vertical and horizontal rectangles and lines. The colors have been limited to black, white, gray, and one of the primary colors, red. This would be a good choice of project for a beginner, because it uses whole squares and gently introduces you to cutting the squares in half. If you are updating an existing table, make sure that you paint the legs with black paint and varnish to give a sleek, lacquer finish.

USING THE TEMPLATE

Trace the template at the back of the book using tracing paper. Turn the tracing paper over and draw over the outline of the design on the reverse in pencil. Turn it back over and place it on top of some brown paper. Trace over the lines once again, transferring the design onto the brown paper. If you are using an existing table, as in the example pictured here, you may find that the template does not cover the full tabletop. If so, use the direct method on page 10 to add a border around the template design, which should be positioned in the center.

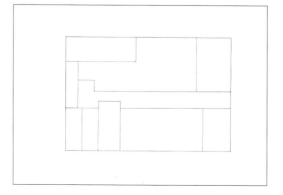

1 Using sandpaper and a block, sand the surface of the tabletop. Then prime it with PVA glue, using a paintbrush. If you are updating an old table, ask at your hardware store which adhesive and primer will work best with the materials.

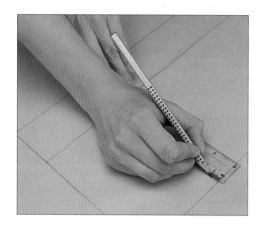

2 Trace the template design onto brown paper. Turn the paper over and mark a center point, using a ruler and pencil, to ensure that the template is in the center when you stick it down onto the table.

3 Cut the pebble gray, shiny black, and charcoal tesserae in half using mosaic nippers (see page 8 for an explanation of the cutting technique and page 7 for safety advice). Leave the red and white mosaics whole. Then, using a damp sponge on gummed brown paper or gum glue on plain brown paper, stick the tesserae into position face down. Complete the pattern and allow to dry.

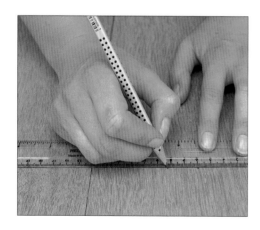

4 If your existing tabletop is larger than the template, mark a cross in the center of the table. This should match the center point drawn on the brown paper in step 2. Draw in the full template rectangle: 24in (60cm) long x 16in (40cm) wide.

5 Mix some adhesive and spread it inside the drawn rectangle using a trowel. Groove the adhesive with a notched edge of the trowel and place the mosaics that you stuck to the brown paper into the adhesive, paper side up.

6 If your table is larger than the template, use the direct method to place pebble gray mosaics, face up, into some adhesive around the edges of the table to give it a neat border.

7 Wet the brown paper with a damp sponge and peel it off the mosaics; make sure you remove all of the paper. Then use an awl or similar tool to prick out any adhesive that has seeped over the edge of the mosaics—this would show through the grout if left in place. Wash the table with a damp sponge immediately afterwards.

8 Mix some gray grout and apply it using a grout float, making sure that you push the grout into all the gaps. When you have finished, remove the excess grout with a damp sponge and polish the table with a dry cloth. Allow to dry for 24 hours.

HINTS AND TIPS

▶ It is advisable to cut the brown paper to the exact size and shape needed before sticking on the tesserae.

▶ To free the tesserae from the sheets on which they are supplied, soak them in warm water; you'll find that this will dissolve the glue and they will then be ready to use.

▶ Read pages 7, 8, and 9 for information on cutting and mixing and advice on safety before starting this project.

▶ If your table is larger than the template but you do not want to add a border to the design, you could extend the lines to the outer edges of the table. You would either have to redraw the design to fit the table or complete the central section and then extend the lines of the design outward.

▶ If you are commissioning a new table for use outside, use marine plywood for the top and galvanized steel for the base.

▶ Paint the table legs black and varnish them to give a lacquer effect.

INSPIRATIONAL IDEAS

This versatile design could be used elsewhere in the home, perhaps as a backsplash on a kitchen wall or as decoration at the bottom of a Zen-style garden pond.

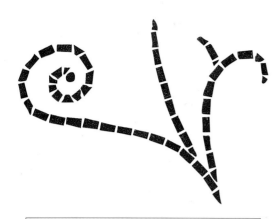

Leaf & Lotus Flower Table

The attractive pattern of Palmette-and-Lotus was traditionally used to decorate all kinds of everyday objects in the Greek household. Palmette is a group of simple leaves arranged in a fan shape, resembling a palm tree leaf; here, it is combined with a lotus flower and linking tendrils to form a stunning overall design. This project is a simplified version of an authentic pattern, using calm, fluid tones of green, turquoise, and ice blue against an off-white background. Applying ivory grout to the mottled white tesserae background gives the tabletop a rustic feel. The pattern itself is easy to complete, since most of it uses half or quarter tesserae, and they are applied using the direct method. The finished table would look wonderful in a sunroom or outside on a patio during the summer.

USING THE TEMPLATE

Trace the template at the back of the book, turn the tracing paper over, and draw over the outline on the reverse in pencil. Turn the tracing back over and position it on the wood. Trace over the front, transferring the design onto the wood. The template only shows a quarter of the design, so you will have to turn it over, re-pencil it, and repeat the tracing four times to complete the circle, matching up the pattern carefully.

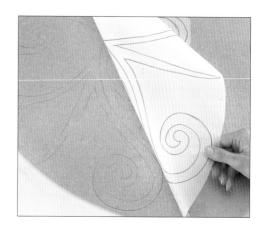

1 Use a pencil, string, and nail to mark out a circle on the particle board, then cut out with a jigsaw (see *Olive Branch Mirror*, pages 44–47, for more detailed instructions). Seal both surfaces and around the edges with waterproof PVA glue.

2 Draw over the design on the back of the template with a pencil. Turn it over and position it on one quarter of the table. Trace over the lines to transfer the design onto the wood.

3 Turn the template over and reposition it, butting it up to the pencil lines you have just marked. Repeat the process in each quarter of the table to form a circle.

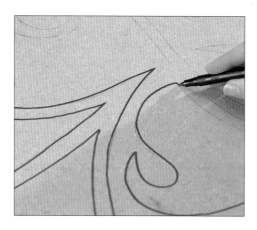

4 The lines do not always show up well on PVA-coated wood, so it is a good idea to draw over them freehand with a marker pen so you can see them clearly when you come to position the tesserae.

5 Cut lots of the green tesserae into halves, and proceeding from the center outward, fill each drawn shape with them. Fill in the other areas with as many whole quarters as you can, and then cut smaller pieces to fit the rest.

6 While you are working, only mix the quantity of adhesive you need for each area so that it does not dry. The background is mainly covered in quarter tesserae. Cut plenty of these, as you will use them up quickly. Work along each shape with sweeping lines so that the background has a rhythm. This project will take several sittings to complete, but it is very satisfying to see the pattern emerging. When you have finished, let the mosaic dry completely.

7 Mix some ivory grout and smear it all over the table. Work it into all the gaps and right up to the edges so that you have a smooth, even surface.

INSPIRATIONAL IDEAS

This design would look equally good on a square

tabletop. You could make the leaf and lotus pattern

in white tiles reversed out of a blue and green

background. You could try mosaicing a half circle

and use it as a plaque above a doorway.

8 Wipe off the excess grout and polish the tabletop with a clean cloth. The tabletop is now ready to slot onto the table base. The base used here is made of galvanized steel so that the table can be used outside.

HINTS AND TIPS

▶ When you work on the turquoise leaf patterns, go from the inside of the table outward. Stick the tesserae in lines as far as you can. For example, on the long leaves, stick a row in the middle first and then up the sides, then fill in the gaps.

▶ Try to end with a row of whole quarters on the outside border. This gives the table a tidy, clean edge.

▶ Fill in the background one section at a time.

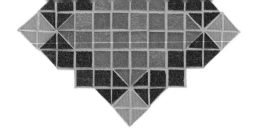

Moroccan-style Geometric Tabletop

Moroccan-style Geometric Tabletop

The art of mosaic in Morocco has traditionally been passed down from father to son for many centuries. Religion dictates that design throughout Morocco depicts no living thing, so geometric design dominates all forms of decoration. For this reason, Moroccan mosaic makers have always been talented mathematicians as well as incredible craftsmen. This tabletop pattern is a stunning example of skilled geometry. The scale is designed to keep the cutting of tiles to a minimum, which makes this project extremely easy to make, and complementary shades of lilac and amethyst contrast effectively with a vibrant lime citrus. A plywood tabletop is used in conjunction with a simply constructed linear iron base; together they make the ideal setting for a Moroccan mint tea party.

TOOLS AND MATERIALS

Tracing paper
Gummed brown paper, or plain brown paper and gum glue
Pencil and ruler
Glass tesserae: ¾ x ¾in (2 x 2cm); quarter sheet of lime, one-and-a-half sheets of dark amethyst, three sheets of lilac, and one sheet of rich amethyst (for the border)
Tile cutters
Surgical and rubber gloves
Safety glasses and mask
PVA glue
Fine paintbrush
Craft knife
Plywood: 2ft (60cm) long x 2ft (60cm) wide x ½in (1cm) deep
Two buckets for mixing
Gray exterior powder adhesive and additive
Trowel
Notched trowel: ¼in (3mm)
Sponge
Awl or similar tool
Gray exterior powder grout and additive
Squeegee
Cloth
Metal table base

GLASS TESSERAE COLORS

Lime citrus
Dark amethyst
Soft lilac
Rich amethyst

USING THE TEMPLATE

Trace the template at the back of the book, turn the tracing paper over, and draw over the outline on the reverse in pencil. Turn the tracing back over and position it on some brown paper. Trace over the front, transferring the design onto the paper.

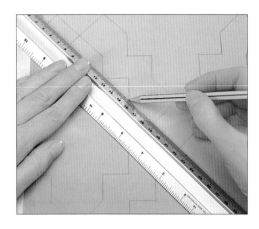
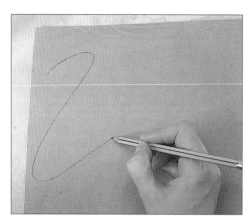

1 Trace the design from the template onto brown paper. Use a ruler to ensure straight lines. You might find it useful to stick the template onto the paper with low-tack tape to stop it from moving around while you are tracing.

2 Turn over the brown paper and draw an unbroken line from left to right across the paper. By doing this, when you come to stick the mosaic onto the plywood, you will have clear registration marks to help you match up the four sections.

3 Cut the tesserae for the whole project. The lime citrus tiles need to be scored and snapped into triangles. The border is a combination of one row of whole tiles and one row of a half tiles, so cut some half tiles, too.

5 Once all the tiles are stuck in position, use a craft knife to cut the paper into quarters. Turn the sections over so they are still in the right position and make sure all the pencil lines on the reverse correspond with the original layout.

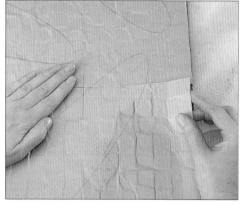

4 Using a damp sponge on gummed brown paper or gum glue on plain brown paper, stick the tiles face down onto the traced design. Work in sections. If your triangles are not 100 percent accurate, you may need to trim them carefully with tile cutters, shaving off any excess.

6 Prime the plywood with PVA glue and allow to dry. Then, using a notched trowel, apply adhesive. Position each section of the mosaic on the plywood, checking that the tiles do not hang over the edge.

7 Wet the back of the brown paper with a sponge and let the water soak in before peeling off the paper. Do not rush this process or the tiles will lift off with the paper; wait until it peels off easily. Some tiles may move slightly when the paper is removed—simply reposition these as you go. Prick out any excess adhesive from between the tesserae with an awl or similar tool.

8 Wearing protective gloves, mix some grout (see page 9). Spread it between the tiles using a squeegee to push the grout into all the spaces. Wipe off any excess grout and clean the surface with a damp sponge. A fine layer of residue will remain, but this will be cleaned off when you give the mosaic a final polish. With the aid of a friend, lift and lower the mosaic onto the metal table base.

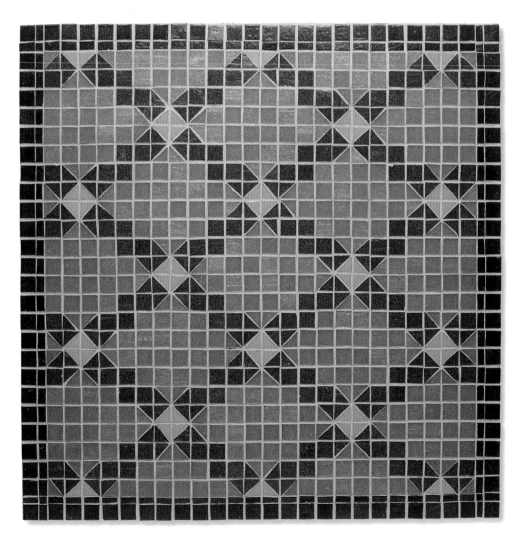

HINTS AND TIPS

▶ Be sure to wear a filter mask when cutting tesserae to give protection against dust particles that can irritate your lungs.

▶ Dilute water-soluble PVA glue in a ratio of 3 parts glue to 2 parts water.

▶ Use a trowel to apply adhesive to large areas such as this repetitive geometric design.

▶ When removing the design from the brown paper, you may have to repeat the wetting process several times before the paper comes away easily.

▶ The wooden tabletop should be a fraction of an inch smaller than the metal frame to allow space for grout.

INSPIRATIONAL IDEAS

The base for this table was specially designed, but you could just as easily use an old iron table from a salvage yard. Simply drill a piece of plywood, cut it to fit the existing tabletop, and screw it in place. For outside use, cover the plywood with a protective coating.

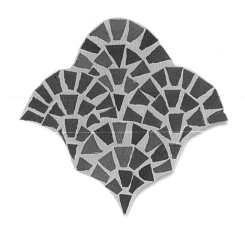

Shell-effect Baseboard

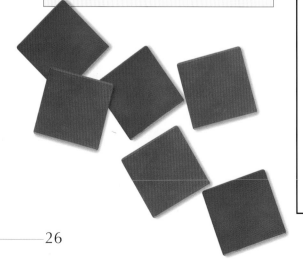

This elaborate and ancient pattern, found throughout Morocco, creates a delicate, lattice effect along the length of a baseboard. It appears complicated but is incredibly easy to create. The key to success is to cut plenty of small triangles before you start working on the design. The basic shell pattern is built up from glossy burgundy and dark green porcelain tiles, which are set off with a beige grout. The shiny, reflective surface of the tiles is enhanced by the matte finish of the grout. When your baseboard is complete and in place, you will find that the surface shines and glistens, picking up and reflecting light. It shimmers and sparkles. Do not feel limited to using this design just along a baseboard: it would work equally well decorating a picture frame or garden steps to evoke an exotic ambience.

USING THE TEMPLATE

Trace the template at the back of the book, turn the tracing paper over, and draw over the outline on the reverse in pencil. Turn it back over and place it over the particle board. Trace over the front, transferring the design onto the board. You will need to reuse this template to create enough sections to cover the length of the baseboard.

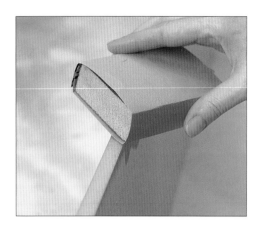

1 Take each section of wood and sand the edges. Apply two coats of PVA glue to the wood. Drill a hole in all four corners of each section of wood, then drill over the hole with a countersink bit. This will prevent the screws from protruding.

2 Trace the design from the template and transfer it onto each wood section using a pencil. Tracing onto a surface that has been covered with PVA can be difficult, so you may need to retrace the marks freehand to make them easier to see.

3 Score lines along each tile using the blade of the tile cutters, then use the snapper part to break them into strips. Remember to wear protective goggles in case of flying splinters and a mask to stop the inhalation of tile dust.

4 Secure each strip between the blades of the mosaic nippers and cut at a 45° angle one way and 45° the other. This creates little V-shaped pieces with flat bottoms, ready to form the arches within the shell shape.

5 Draw a shell shape on a piece of paper and practice positioning the tesserae. This way you will know roughly how many pieces are required for each arch. This is not a precise science and each section must be treated as a separate space.

6 Mix a quantity of adhesive (see page 9) and trowel it neatly onto one shell shape. Position the tesserae, piece by piece, beginning at the top of the shell. This way you work in arches from top to bottom. It is important that there are the same number of rows and a single piece at the bottom of each shell shape.

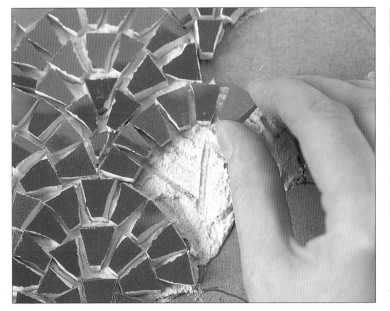

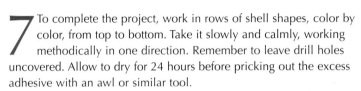

7 To complete the project, work in rows of shell shapes, color by color, from top to bottom. Take it slowly and calmly, working methodically in one direction. Remember to leave drill holes uncovered. Allow to dry for 24 hours before pricking out the excess adhesive with an awl or similar tool.

8 Mix some grout (see page 9) and trowel it into the gaps. Clean off the excess with a damp sponge. Wearing protective gloves, smooth the grout with your fingers over the top edge of the baseboard so that the wood is covered and it is slightly domed: this adds to the rustic, Moroccan look. Allow the grout to dry for 24 hours. For attaching the mosaic to the wall, see *Hints and Tips* (below).

HINTS AND TIPS

▶ Tile cutters are the best tool for cutting tiles of this size, as they score a guideline before making the cut. Scoring weakens the tile so that it breaks exactly where you want and not randomly at an angle.

▶ You will need to prepare many more tesserae than you might think for this project—the edges of most tiles are slightly beveled making them unsuitable for this pattern, so there will be some wastage.

▶ Once your grout is dry, fix the mosaic to the wall. With an electric drill, drill holes in the wall in the same position as those in the mosaic and fit plastic wall anchors, then screw the mosaic in place. Mix a small amount of adhesive and stick the tesserae over the area covering the screws. Allow to dry for 24 hours. Prick out excess adhesive with an awl, grout, wipe clean, and polish.

INSPIRATIONAL IDEAS

This pattern lends itself to experimentation with different color combinations. Creating each shell shape in a different color scheme would produce a vibrant and very modern mosaic. This design would work well for a floor mosaic—just reuse the template to create a repeating pattern.

Birds & Flowers Wall Plaque

Why not re-create a decorative mosaic that can be displayed like a painting? This delicate mosaic design of birds and flowers will form a stunning centerpiece for any room and promote feelings of peace and tranquillity. The Romans were great observers of life and nature, and many of their designs featured animals and plants. Inspired by this theme, this project captures the beauty of the natural world. It was created using the direct mosaic-laying method (see page 10). Unpolished marble and a palette of natural earthy colors were selected to give an authentic rustic look. Finally, a warm beige grout was applied, which tones in with the background color, encouraging the detail to stand out. This wall plaque was professionally framed, but you could also paint the edges in a contrasting color to create a softer look.

USING THE TEMPLATE

Trace the template at the back of the book, turn the tracing paper over, and draw over the outline on the reverse in pencil. Turn it back over and place it over the plywood. Trace over the front, transferring the design onto the board. The flower and bird are repeated to create the whole pattern. Simply reuse the template to trace the other bird and flowers.

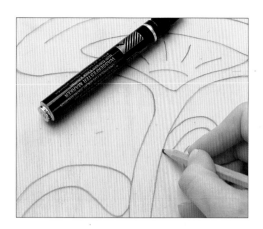

1 Drill a hole in each corner of the plywood, then drill over the four holes using a countersink bit. Remove any rough edges with sandpaper and a block.

2 Use a paintbrush to coat the surface and edges of the plywood with PVA glue, and allow to dry. Cut the marble tesserae with a hammer and hardy (see page 8). Use whole squares for the background and finer pieces for the details.

3 Trace the design onto the plywood (see *Using the Template*). When the image is complete, draw over the outlines with a marker pen. These lines will make the design easier to follow and will be hidden when the tesserae are stuck in position.

4 Mix some powder adhesive. Apply adhesive onto the back of each tessera with a palette knife, and follow the outline of the birds with one row of tesserae before filling in the body. Complete the flowers in the same way.

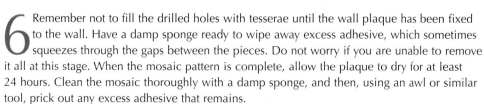

5 Once the details are complete, start on the background. For this section, apply the adhesive, smooth with a trowel, and then make grooves in the surface using a notched trowel. Start sticking the tesserae in place, working across the board in rows.

6 Remember not to fill the drilled holes with tesserae until the wall plaque has been fixed to the wall. Have a damp sponge ready to wipe away excess adhesive, which sometimes squeezes through the gaps between the pieces. Do not worry if you are unable to remove it all at this stage. When the mosaic pattern is complete, allow the plaque to dry for at least 24 hours. Clean the mosaic thoroughly with a damp sponge, and then, using an awl or similar tool, prick out any excess adhesive that remains.

7 Before grouting, brush a sealant onto the marble with a clean brush. This will protect the marble from the grout, which may discolor it. Mix 3 parts white grout with 1 part beige grout to create a subtle tone. Apply the grout to the whole mosaic with a float. Push it into the gaps between the tesserae as you work across the board. Wipe away excess with a damp sponge and polish with a soft, dry cloth. Allow to dry for 24 hours, then apply another coat of sealant.

8 To fix the plaque in position, drill holes in the wall where you want the plaque to hang and insert plastic wall anchors. Attach the plaque to the wall using a drill to fix the screws. Once it is in place, mix a small amount of adhesive, and stick the tesserae over the blank area covering the screws. Allow to dry for at least 24 hours. Prick out, apply a coat of sealant, grout, wipe, and polish. When this is dry, apply a final coat of sealant.

HINTS AND TIPS

❯ It is advisable to cut a large number of tesserae before you start to lay them, so that you do not have to stop mid-flow.

❯ Always work in well-ventilated conditions when mixing adhesives and grout, and if necessary, wear a mouth and nose filter to protect yourself from fumes.

❯ Use a palette knife to apply adhesive to small areas, such as the flowers and birds, and a notched trowel to cover large areas, such as the background.

❯ Notice the halo effect around the details of the bird and flowers. This is a Roman device called "*Opus Vermiculatum*." Derived from the Latin for worm, "*vermis*," the tesserae follow the lines of the pattern like a worm.

INSPIRATIONAL IDEAS

If you find this large wall plaque too ambitious, make a smaller plaque featuring just one bird and flower. This image would work well in any room, or would be perfect mounted on a garden wall.

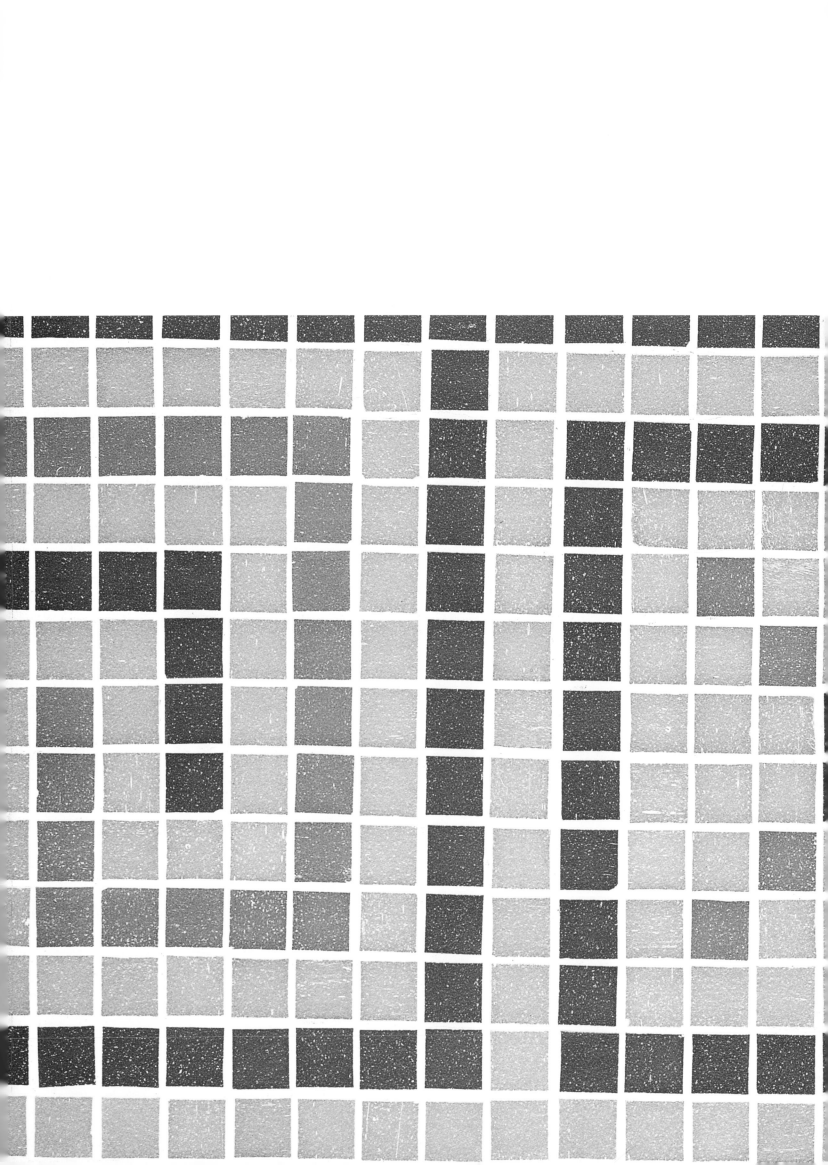

KITCHENS & BATHROOMS

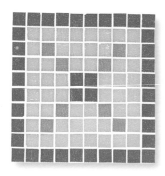

Greek Key Design Bathmat

The key motif is one of the most instantly recognizable Greek designs. Its simple, repeating pattern runs in a continuous, seemingly endless line. The key was typically used as an edging for elaborate designs on pottery and chiseled into sculptures, as well as featuring as a detail on clothing and jewelry. Throughout ancient and modern Greece, it appears widely—on ornaments in the home, on the surrounding magnificent architecture, and even as a linear border on traditional Greek costumes. This project is simple to make because there is no cutting of tesserae involved, and the indirect method is used to apply the tiles to the wooden base of the bathmat. The combination of pale blues and aqua sets the scene for a peaceful, tranquil refuge in your bathroom.

USING THE TEMPLATE

Trace the template at the back of the book, turn the tracing paper over, and draw over the outline on the reverse in pencil. Turn the tracing back over and position it on the brown paper. Trace over the front, transferring the design onto the brown paper. For this particular design, it helps to shade in the pattern so that you can see clearly where the tesserae should be positioned. They are applied using the indirect method (see page 11 for instructions).

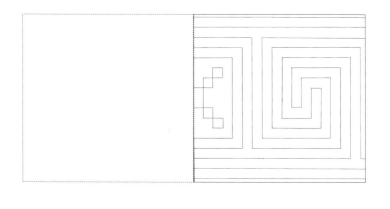

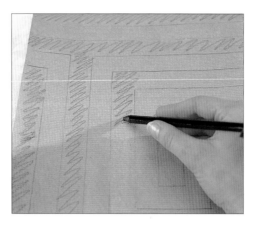
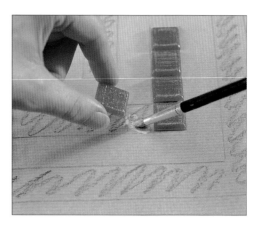

1 First, paint the front, back, and sides of the wood with two coats of waterproof PVA glue to seal it. This is essential if you are going to use the mat in a bathroom or it will eventually absorb water, expand, and start to disintegrate, even if you have used exterior-grade wood.

2 Transfer the template onto the brown paper (see instructions on page 36). You will now have a faint linear image on the brown paper. Using a pencil, shade in the pattern so that it will be easy to where the tesserae should be positioned.

3 Using a damp sponge on gummed brown paper or gum glue on plain brown paper, stick the tesserae into position face down. Try to keep the gaps between the tiles equal so that the grout will look regular and even.

5 Apply adhesive to the wood using a notched trowel and gently lower each half of the design into place. Next, using a small trowel, apply adhesive onto the backs of the darkest tesserae and stick them one by one onto the edges of the board, being careful not to disturb the pattern.

4 Now fill in the background color so the design is complete and you are ready to stick the tiles to the wood. Turn the paper over and draw a few lines across the back. Cut the pattern in half with a craft knife so that you have two smaller sections—these will be easier to maneuve. The lines you drew on the back will enable you to align the two pattern pieces accurately when you put them in position on the particle board base.

6 Allow to dry for 24 hours. Wet the brown paper with a damp sponge and wait for it to soak in. The paper should peel off easily in two sections. If any tiles come loose, stick them down again.

7 Wait for the adhesive to dry. Some of it might seep through and stick out above the tiles. Using an awl or similar tool to prick out the excess, then dust away the dry adhesive. You are now ready to grout.

HINTS AND TIPS

▶ If this is your first attempt, draw a rough sketch of the grid to help you position the tiles.

▶ Don't try to peel off the paper too soon—it takes longer to dry than you might think.

▶ You may want to stick on rubber feet to raise the bathmat off the ground slightly so that water has less chance to seep in.

▶ You could use a wooden molding as edging instead of tiles.

8 Mix the grout and spread it over the whole mosaic. Disperse it with a squeegee or trowel, and work it into the gaps. Use your fingers to neaten the grout around the outside of the design. You may need to wait for the outside edges to dry and regrout to get a good edge. Polish the mosaic with a cloth and the project is complete.

INSPIRATIONAL IDEAS

By using quarter tiles you can shrink the design to make a pretty border running along the top of a

baseboard or at chair rail height, or an attractive surround for a mirror.

Rustic Fish Tablemat

TOOLS AND MATERIALS

Exterior-grade particle board:
11in (57cm) long x 15in (37.5cm)
wide x 1in (2.5cm) deep
Waterproof PVA glue
Paintbrush
Gummed brown paper, or plain
brown paper and gum glue
Tracing paper and pencil
Fine paintbrush
Marker pen
Glass tesserae:
¾ x ¾in (2 x 2cm)
Mirror tesserae
Two buckets
Trowel
Notched trowel: ¼in (3mm)
White exterior powder adhesive
White external powder grout
Safety glasses and mask
Sponge and squeegee
Cloth
Mosaic nippers
Tile cutters
Awl or similar tool

GLASS TESSERAE COLORS

White
Dark blue
Mid blue
Mirror tesserae

The sea features strongly in the legends of ancient Greece, and it has always been at the center of Greek culture. So much of Greece and its islands is surrounded by water that ships, fish, and all thing aquatic have had a huge influence on Greek designs for all kinds of everyday objects. Many of the houses are whitewashed and stand in stark contrast with the blue Mediterranean sky and sea, forming the typical Greek color palette. This project combines the white and blue color scheme with a fish design highlighted with mirror tesserae. The project can be tackled in many ways: the shapes of tesserae used to fill the design are only a suggestion, and you could use any shapes you like. The tesserae are applied to the wood using the indirect method, then a border is stuck down by the direct method.

USING THE TEMPLATE

Trace the template at the back of the book, turn the tracing paper over, and draw over the outline on the reverse in pencil. Turn the tracing back over and position it on the brown paper. Trace over the front, transferring the design onto the brown paper. You may wish to draw over this outline again in marker pen to make sure it is clearly visible when you come to stick down the tesserae.

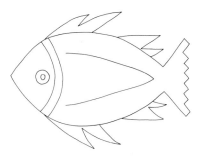

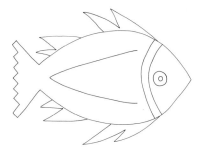

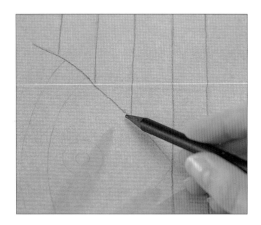

1 Trace the template onto the brown paper, then draw over the pencil line with marker pen. (The pencil line always seems a bit too faint and you can work more quickly with a clearer design.)

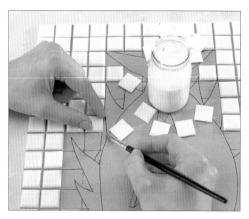

2 First, stick down all the whole white tiles that require no cutting. It can be easier to draw a square grid for the white tiles so that you can position them quickly and accurately.

3 Cut lots of half tesserae and nip them into squares, ready for the body of the fish. Next, nibble a square into a tiny circle to form the eye. Read the advice about cutting on page 8 before you start.

4 Cutting the mirror tiles is easier than you may think. All you have to do is score them and then snap. Cut them into halves and squares and then little rectangles to go round the fishes' eyes.

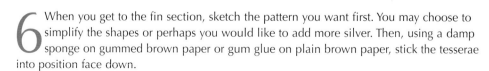

5 Fill in the eye of the fish first and then the rest of the head. Insert a line of silver mirror tesserae to add shimmer and shine to the finished project.

6 When you get to the fin section, sketch the pattern you want first. You may choose to simplify the shapes or perhaps you would like to add more silver. Then, using a damp sponge on gummed brown paper or gum glue on plain brown paper, stick the tesserae into position face down.

7 Finish all the blue and silver areas, then start to fill in the white tiles, nipping off sections to fit the holes. Allow all this to dry and trim the edges of the paper, ready to stick it to the wood.

8 Seal the wood with waterproof PVA glue, then apply the adhesive with a notched trowel. Gently lower the fishes into place and push the panel into the adhesive.

9 Carefully stick individual tiles around the outside to form a neat edge, applying adhesive to each tile and holding the tile in place for a few seconds.

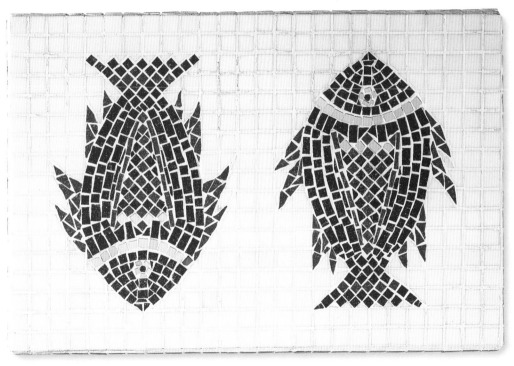

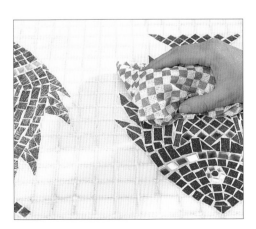

10 When it has dried, soak off the brown paper, pick out excess adhesive, grout, and polish.

HINTS AND TIPS

▶ Try out a different combination of patterns and colors on paper first to help you decide on the effect you want.

▶ It might be a good idea to back the mosaic with felt or rubber feet to prevent it from scratching the tabletop or other surface you plan to use it on.

INSPIRATIONAL IDEAS

The fish design would also look wonderful in a bathroom, swimming on the wall around a bathtub, or as a backsplash behind a basin. See pages 96–99 for instructions on how to make a wall frieze.

Olive Branch Mirror

TOOLS AND MATERIALS

Ceramic tesserae:
9/10 x 9/10in (23 x 23mm)
Two pieces of particle board:
24in (60cm) long x 24in (60cm)
wide x 1/2in (12mm) deep
Jigsaw
Mirror to fit the hole
PVA glue
Paintbrush
Tracing paper
Pencil, string, and nail
Tape measure
Workbench and clamps
Mosaic nippers
White powder adhesive
Beige powder grout
Safety glasses and mask
Trowel and palette knife
Gloves
Two buckets
Squeegee and clean cloths

CERAMIC TESSERAE COLORS

Brown
Green
Blue
Red
White

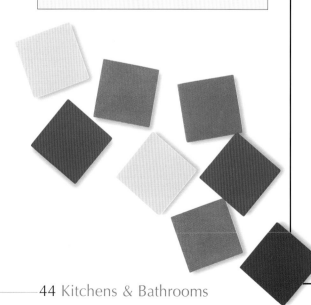

Greece is renowned for its abundance of olive trees and excellent olive oil. Olives are a symbol of hope, peace, and general wellbeing, so they are a natural choice for a Greek mosaic project. The gently curving branches in olive green, highlighted with blue leaves and plump, chocolate-colored olives, combine to create a warm, Mediterranean feel. The mirror will make a beautiful feature in the bathroom, but can also be used for hallways, living rooms, or bedrooms. This project is quite time-consuming, but you will soon figure out how to cut all the odd-shaped pieces you need. You can either cut each tile to fit a specific place, or cut lots of tiles and move them around like a jigsaw puzzle until you find a place where each fits. Don't throw away any off-cuts as there is bound to be a place for them.

USING THE TEMPLATE

Trace the template at the back of the book, turn the tracing paper over, and draw over the outline on the reverse in pencil. Turn the tracing back over and position it on the frame. Trace over the front, transferring the design onto the frame. The template only shows half of the design, so you will have to turn it over, re-pencil it, and repeat the tracing to complete the circle, joining the edges carefully so the pattern appears seamless.

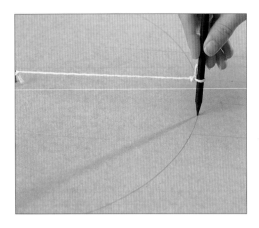

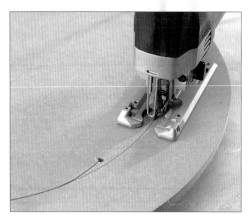

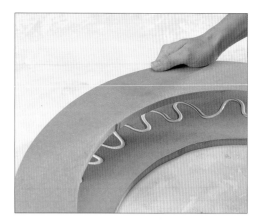

1 Draw a 23in (59cm) diameter circle on each piece of wood (see *Hints and Tips*). On the first piece, draw another circle 4in (11cm) in from the edge. This is the front. On the second piece, draw a circle 2in (5cm) in from the edge. This is the back.

2 Cut around the outside of the bigger circles, then drill a hole on the inside of the lines large enough to fit the jigsaw blade. Guide the jigsaw around until you have two rings.

3 Liberally apply PVA glue to one of the rings and then clamp them together and allow to dry. Then cover the whole frame, back and front, with PVA glue to seal the wood. Wash your brush immediately after use.

5 To cut out the olives, take a tessera and cut it in half with mosaic nippers. Cut again into quarters and then nibble the edges until you have little, round shapes.

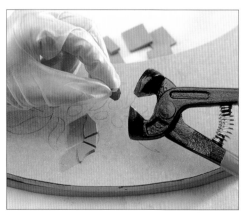

4 Trace the design from the template onto the front of the frame. The template only shows half the design, so when you have completed one side, turn over the template, re-pencil it, and repeat the tracing. If you turn the tracing and do not re-pencil, your branches will face different directions. Both ways look good. The choice is yours.

6 To make the leaves, cut tiles in half and then at an angle to make triangles. Mix some adhesive and stick all the leaves, stalks, and olives in place a section at a time. Allow them to dry.

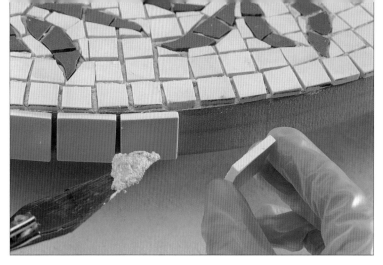

7 Fill in the background lines with as many quarter tiles as possible, then fill in the gaps. Apply adhesive to the backs of the tesserae and stick whole tiles around the outside edge and quarter tiles on the inside edge. Allow to dry for 24 hours.

8 Prick out any excess adhesive with an awl or similar tool and wipe away any dust. Then apply beige grout. Wipe off the excess with a squeegee and polish with a clean cloth. Use a slightly damp cloth for the first clean and a dry one for the second.

HINTS AND TIPS

▶ To draw the circles on the pieces of wood, mark the center of the wood with a dot, and tie your pencil onto the end of the string. Attach a nail to the string 11½in (29.5cm) from the pencil and gently tap the nail into the center dot. Hold the string tight and draw the circles, keeping the pencil upright on the wood.

▶ When you fill in the background, start with the edges and work inward. That way, you can use as many whole quarters as possible. The rest of the background is made up of quarters and offcuts.

▶ To make the stalk pieces, cut a red tessera in half and then cut it again lengthwise. It should split unevenly, just as you want it. If you find this hard, score and snap the lines.

INSPIRATIONAL IDEAS

This design would look great as a border in a

shower or along the back of kitchen cabinets.

You could make a square mirror instead, with

each side using two branches that face in

opposite directions.

Cool Blue Backsplash

Cool Blue
Backsplash

This stylish backsplash has been created from glazed ceramic tiles with a glossy surface in soothing turquoise, sky blue, and brilliant white. Blue and white were the original colors of ancient Moroccan mosaic, a palette brought from China by the Persians. Here, they combine to produce a tranquil, peaceful bathroom. Created by laying tiles on the diagonal, this eye-catching pattern looks impressive but is simple to follow and requires little cutting. The ceramic tiles used here come with mesh on the back rather than paper. You can cut the sheets into sections and lay the mosaics in chunks or remove the backing altogether and use each tile individually. Whichever method you use, you will find this a quick and easy project that creates a stunning result.

TOOLS AND MATERIALS

Mottled ceramic tiles:
1 x 1in (2.5 x 2.5cm);
one sheet of each color
Exterior-grade plywood:
26in (65cm) long x 18in (43cm)
wide x ½in (1cm) deep
Electric drill and
countersink bit
Waterproof PVA glue
Paintbrush
Tracing paper
Pencil
Ruler
Tile cutters
Surgical and rubber gloves
Safety glasses and mask
Two buckets for mixing
White exterior powder adhesive
and additive
Trowel
Awl or similar tool
White exterior powder grout
and additive
Squeegee
Sponge
Cloth
Plastic wall anchors and screws

CERAMIC TILE COLORS

Brilliant white
Sky blue
Turquoise

USING THE TEMPLATE

Trace the template at the back of the book, turn the tracing paper over, and draw over the outline on the reverse in pencil. Turn it back over and place it over the plywood. Trace over the front, transferring your design onto the board.

The blue tile border is not incorporated in the template and space should be allowed for it around the edge of the plywood.

1 Take your chosen tiles and try varying their position within the square design. It is amazing how different the project can look by simply changing the colors around. Put together a number of designs and choose a favorite from these.

2 Using exterior-grade plywood as the base, drill a hole in each corner. Then drill each of the holes with a countersink bit. Brush two coats of waterproof PVA glue on the front and back of the board to prime the surface.

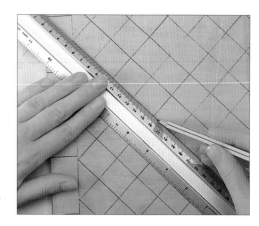

3 Trace the design from the template directly onto the board. If the pattern is very faint, draw over the pencil line by hand. Use a ruler to ensure straight lines. Sticking down the template to hold it in place can help when tracing.

4 Count up the number of triangle pieces needed for the design. Score each tile using the tile cutters and snap in two. A quick precise action gives a much neater line than a slow cut – perhaps buy a few extra tiles to allow for mistakes.

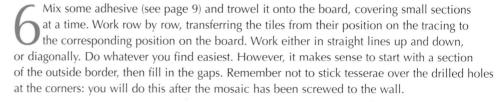

5 Remove the tiles from the sheets and group them into color piles. Spread out the tracing and lay the tiles in place, ready for sticking to the board. The more accurate your placings at this stage, the quicker the project will be finished.

6 Mix some adhesive (see page 9) and trowel it onto the board, covering small sections at a time. Work row by row, transferring the tiles from their position on the tracing to the corresponding position on the board. Work either in straight lines up and down, or diagonally. Do whatever you find easiest. However, it makes sense to start with a section of the outside border, then fill in the gaps. Remember not to stick tesserae over the drilled holes at the corners: you will do this after the mosaic has been screwed to the wall.

7 When the whole board is complete, check for any protruding tiles on the border, and if necessary, reposition them against the edge. Prick out loose adhesive with an awl or similar tool while it is still wet—you may have to do this section by section. (As this is a large project, you may not have time to complete the task in one sitting, but do not be tempted to leave any adhesive.)

8 Mix the grout (see page 9) and smear it on with a palette knife, making sure you fill all the gaps. Wipe clean the surface with a wet sponge. Allow to dry for 24 hours. Polish off the dusty residue from the surface with a dry cloth. See *Hints and Tips* (below) for instructions on how to fix the mosaic to the wall.

HINTS AND TIPS

▶ To help decide on the final color configuration, hold a mirror against each square design—this will double the effect and give an idea of its repetitive appeal.

▶ This project uses large tesserae, although you could use standard-size tiles if the template is scaled down. You can do this by reducing the design on a photocopier. Remember that the plywood needs to match the new template size.

▶ There can be a lot of color variation in mottled tiles. When two or four tiles are linked together, check that none of them is much lighter or darker than the others.

▶ If small holes appear when rubbing off the excess grout, simply run your finger along the grouted line to fill them in.

▶ After drilling holes in the wall where you want your backsplash to go, and inserting plastic wall anchors, screw the mosaic to the wall. Then mix a small amount of adhesive, and stick the tesserae over the area covering the screws. Allow to dry for 24 hours. Prick out excess adhesive, then grout and wipe as described above.

INSPIRATIONAL IDEAS

This pattern could be adapted to work on a much larger surface—a shower basin or bathroom floor, for example. Simply reuse the template, repeating the design over a larger area.

Vibrant Star Water Bowl

TOOLS AND MATERIALS

Flat-bottomed terra-cotta bowl:
16in (40cm) diameter
Waterproof PVA glue
Paintbrush
Tracing paper
Gummed brown paper, or plain
brown paper and gum glue
Pencil and scissors
Glass tesserae: ¾ x ¾in (2 x 2cm);
one sheet of red, half sheet of
black and deep orange, and three-
quarter sheet of tangerine orange
Tile cutters
Surgical and rubber gloves
Safety glasses and mask
Fine paintbrush
Two buckets for mixing
Black exterior powder adhesive
and additive
Notched trowel: ¼in (3mm)
Trowel
Sponge
Awl or similar tool tool
Masking tape
Black exterior powder grout
and additive
Squeegee
Cloth

GLASS TESSERAE COLORS

Jet black
Tangerine orange
Deep orange
Blood red

Decorate a plain bowl with intensely colored glass tesserae, in a palette that evokes the exotic spice markets of Marrakesh. The intricate design works harmoniously with the bright hues, whereas the contrasting black grout highlights the colors. Although the pattern is quite complicated, if you tackle small sections at a time it is easily achieved, and as the overall project is quite small, it does not take long to complete. To relax away from the bustle of everyday life, Moroccans often sit in the sanctuary of cool courtyards and float aromatic rose petals and flowers in their fountains. Emulate this custom by filling this stunning bowl with water and floating your own choice of blooms. Or you might prefer to float scented candles across the surface to set the scene for a candlelit Moroccan dinner.

USING THE TEMPLATE

Trace the template at the back of the book, turn the tracing paper over, and draw over the outline on the reverse in pencil. Turn the tracing back over and position it on brown paper. Trace over the front, transferring the design onto the brown paper. Cut out the bowl shape, so that it fits inside the bowl.

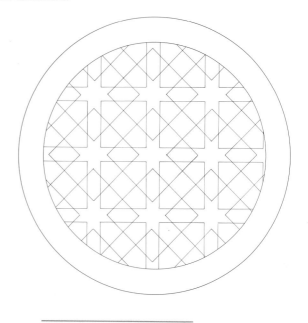

For a different size bowl, you will have to reduce or enlarge the template accordingly to fit.

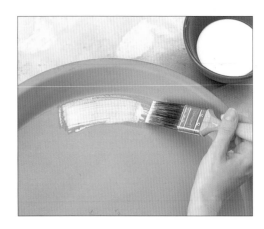

1 Give the terra-cotta bowl two coats of PVA glue, inside and out, to make it water-resistant. Terra-cotta is very porous, so test how watertight the bowl is by filling it with water and leaving it on the side of a sink to see if the water seeps through.

2 Trace the template from the back of the book and transfer it onto brown paper. Using tile cutters, cut the tiles into strips, squares, and triangles (see page 8). Lay out the tesserae on the pattern before you start gluing, as this is a complicated design.

3 Each space of this design requires a different cut of tesserae and so there is a lot of nipping, scoring, and snapping to do. You may find cutting tricky at first but it does become easier as you proceed. Then, using a damp sponge on gummed brown paper or gum glue on plain brown paper, stick the tesserae into position face down. Complete the pattern and allow them to dry.

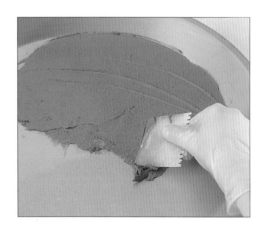

4 Mix a quantity of adhesive and smear it on the base of the bowl using the flat side of the trowel—if any sticks to the upright edge, clean it off. Smooth the surface evenly, then use the notched side of the trowel to make grooves in it.

5 Carefully lower the entire circle onto the adhesive, butting it up to the edges. Once the whole circle is down, gently wiggle the tiles into the adhesive to make sure they are grounded. Put aside for 24 hours to allow the adhesive to set.

6 Wet the paper with a sponge and gently peel it away from the tiles (you may need to keep wetting the paper). Some tiles may stay on the paper—peel them off and stick them on separately.

7 To mosaic the upright edge, apply adhesive to whole red tiles and push them into place. Make sure there is a gap surrounding each tile for the grout, and that they are spaced as evenly as possible. When the circle is nearly complete, you may need to readjust the spacing between each tile (use only whole tiles). Prick out any excess adhesive from between the tesserae with a bradawl.

8 Stick pieces of masking tape along the top edge of the bowl to make a neat circle. Mix some grout and apply it to the bottom of the bowl and up the sides with a squeegee. Take the grout up to the masked edge and smooth it neatly. When the grout is almost dry, peel off the tape to reveal a neat edge. Allow the grout to set for 24 hours, then polish with a dry cloth.

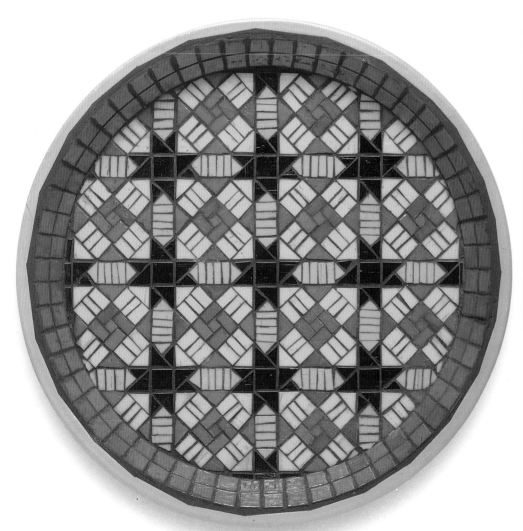

HINTS AND TIPS

▶ Because there are many different shapes in this design and you do not want to waste tiles through miscutting, follow the instructions on page 8 for *Cutting and Scoring*.

▶ It is advisable to cut all the tesserae before you start to lay them so that you do not have to break off mid-flow.

▶ Work in small sections when grouting your mosaic. This will enable you to wipe away any excess before it dries hard.

▶ If you are planning to fill this bowl with water, do not place it directly on a treasured piece of furniture the first time in case any liquid seeps through.

INSPIRATIONAL IDEAS

The vivid color combination chosen for this bowl is typically Moroccan. This intricate design would work in any colour scheme: blues and greens would be especially effective. Remember to use a grout that matches your colors.

Bathroom Frieze Wave Design

TOOLS AND MATERIALS

Pencil and ruler
Level
Polished marble tesserae:
⅝ x ⅝in (1.5 x 1.5cm)
Hammer and hardy
Surgical and rubber gloves
Tracing paper
Gummed brown paper, or plain
brown paper and gum glue
Powder adhesive and additive
Two buckets for mixing
Trowel
Notched trowel: ¼in (3mm)
Sponge
Scissors
Awl or similar tool
Paintbrush
Marble impregnator (optional)
Marble protector (optional)
Gray and white powder grout
and additive
Grout float
Soft cloth
Marble sealant

MARBLE TESSERAE COLORS

Green
White
Black

A dd a touch of elegance to your bathroom with this exquisite border. The wave design, with its crests of water and waves, is a traditional pattern that was commonly used as a border in floor and wall designs in Roman villas throughout Britain. Dating from approximately the first few centuries A.D., this wave design is a timeless classic and would look good in any modern home. This motif is surprisingly easy to re-create using the indirect method (see page 11), and the pattern can be repeated to run around a whole room. Be sure to measure your wall before you start, to ensure that the frieze is straight and at the right height. The strong, simple palette of black, white and sea green marble creates a sophisticated look, while sleek, polished marble lends a touch of luxury.

USING THE TEMPLATE

Trace the template at the back of the book, turn the tracing paper over, and draw over the outline on the reverse in pencil. Turn the tracing paper back over and position it on brown paper. Trace over the outline again, transferring the design onto the brown paper. Repeat until you have the correct length of frieze for your room.

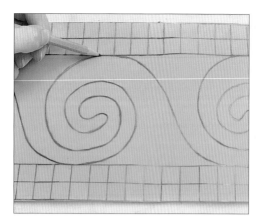

1 Use a level to draw a straight horizontal line along the wall to mark the top of the frieze. Measure down 6¾in (17cm) and draw another horizontal line to mark the bottom of the frieze. Draw these lines to the desired length.

2 Cut the marble with a hammer and hardy (see page 8). This will help to give your marble a good, sharp cut with minimal shattering. The white and green pieces are the only colors that will need to be cut—the black tesserae are used whole.

3 Take the template at the back of the book, and trace the design onto brown paper. Use a paper clip to hold the tracing paper securely in place.

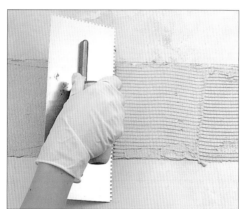

5 Mix some adhesive and spread it onto the wall with a trowel, staying within the pencil guidelines. Then use a notched trowel to groove the bed. If you go over the pencil guidelines, remove the excess adhesive with a damp sponge.

4 Using a damp sponge on gummed brown paper or gum glue on plain brown paper, stick the tesserae into position face down. Start by filling in the top and bottom borders, then move on to the central wave design before tackling the background. Make sure that the tesserae are evenly spaced. Allow the mosaic pieces to dry for 24 hours.

6 Stick the mosaic to the wall, cutting it up if necessary to make it more manageable. Line up the top of the frieze with the top of the adhesive on the wall and carefully stick each section down, without leaving any gaps.

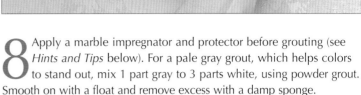

7 When it is dry, moisten the brown paper with a damp sponge and peel it off to reveal the design. Once all the brown paper has been removed, clean the mosaic thoroughly. Using an awl or similar tool, pick out any excess adhesive or residual glue.

8 Apply a marble impregnator and protector before grouting (see *Hints and Tips* below). For a pale gray grout, which helps colors to stand out, mix 1 part gray to 3 parts white, using powder grout. Smooth on with a float and remove excess with a damp sponge.

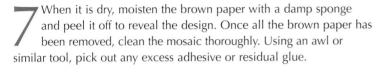

HINTS AND TIPS

◗ If the template at the back of this book is not the right size to fit in your bathroom, reduce or enlarge it on a photocopier.

◗ You can sit or stand when cutting tesserae with a hammer and hardy—just make sure that you are comfortable and that your cutting hand is not restricted in any way.

◗ If you are using plain brown paper and gum glue, make sure that the glue is water-soluble so that you can wash it off in step 7. This is available from art, craft, or hardware stores. If you prefer, you could use wallpaper paste as an alternative.

◗ Before grouting, it is helpful to brush on a marble impregnator, followed by a marble protector. Both are available from tile stores. These protect the marble from dirt and from staining.

◗ When grouting, make sure that you lay drop cloths because the process can be messy.

9 Finally, clean and polish the mosaic with a dry, soft cloth. To maintain the beauty of the marble, there are several acid-free products available that will protect without damaging the marble or the sealant. These products are available from most mosaic suppliers.

INSPIRATIONAL IDEAS

This design can easily be adapted. Try using it to create a mirror frame, or a

border around a tiled floor. It could also be re-created in glass in brighter colors.

Kitchen Backsplash

What could be more stylish in your kitchen than a classical urn that is overflowing with fruits of the vine? While the design is truly Roman, the stylized form, bright colors, and use of glass tesserae give this project a contemporary feel. To provide extra sparkle in this backsplash, the leaves are made from glass tesserae that are marbled with gold leaf. A subtle tone of grout was used for this project to help the details to stand out. Although this mosaic looks elaborate, it is not difficult to make—you can cut most of the glass tesserae into irregular pieces of any shape. You will need to take a little extra care when making the delicate lines of the stalks, which require small tesserae, and the grapes, which need circular pieces.

TOOLS AND MATERIALS

Tape measure
Level
Pencil
Tracing paper
Waterproof PVA glue and paintbrush
Vitreous glass tesserae:
¾ x ¾in (2 x 2cm)
Mosaic nippers
Surgical and rubber gloves
Safety glasses and mask
Adhesive and additive
Two buckets for mixing
Palette knife
Trowel
Notched trowel: ¼in (3mm)
Awl or similar tool
Beige and white powder grout
and additive
Grout float or rubber squeegee
Drop cloth
Sponge
Soft cloth

GLASS TESSERAE COLORS

Butterscotch
Caramel
Toffee
Amethyst
Lilac
Grass green
Mint green
Olive with gold vein
Gray green
Charcoal

USING THE TEMPLATE

Trace the template at the back of the book, turn the tracing paper over, and draw over the outline on the reverse in pencil. Turn it back over and hold it against the wall. Trace over the front, transferring your design onto the wall. To create extra leaves, simply reuse the leaf on the template by moving the template around the wall and retracing the design.

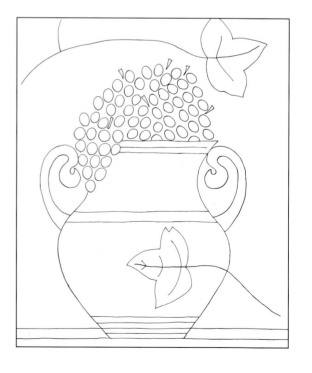

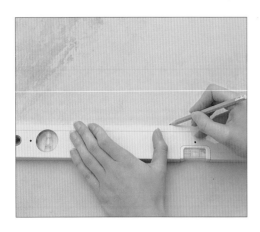

1 Using a tape measure and level, measure the width of the wall. With a pencil, make a small mark halfway across. Measure the height of the area, making another mark exactly halfway. Where these two marks meet is your center point.

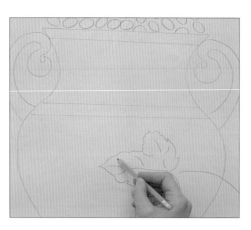

2 Trace the template onto the wall (see *Using the Template* on page 60). Make sure that you line it up with the center point.

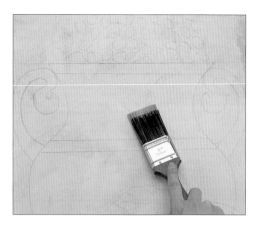

3 Prime the wall with two coats of waterproof PVA glue. While waiting for the glue to dry, start cutting the glass tesserae with mosaic nippers (see page 8). Always wear surgical gloves, safety glasses, and a mask when cutting vitreous glass.

4 Start with the grape area first. Mix some adhesive (see page 9) and apply a small amount to the grape area. Position the grapes firmly into the adhesive. Be sure to wear surgical gloves in order to protect your hands.

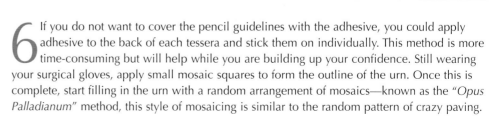

5 Next, work on the leaves. Use a palette knife to apply a small amount of adhesive to the area within the outline. Position the tesserae into the adhesive—work first on the stem, then the veins, and finally the rest of the leaves.

6 If you do not want to cover the pencil guidelines with the adhesive, you could apply adhesive to the back of each tessera and stick them on individually. This method is more time-consuming but will help while you are building up your confidence. Still wearing your surgical gloves, apply small mosaic squares to form the outline of the urn. Once this is complete, start filling in the urn with a random arrangement of mosaics—known as the "*Opus Palladianum*" method, this style of mosaicing is similar to the random pattern of crazy paving.

7 Once the details are complete, start on the background. Use a trowel to apply the adhesive to the wall, then groove the surface with a notched trowel. Position the tesserae, again using the *"Opus Palladianum"* method (see step 6).

8 Complete the effect by mosaicing a charcoal border above and below the design. Allow the mosaic to dry for 24 hours. Then, using an awl or similar tool, carefully remove any excess adhesive or it will show through the grout.

9 Mix the grout until you achieve a medium-thick consistency. The grout that was used for this project was made from 1 part beige powder grout to 3 parts white grout: this creates a subtle tone that matches the color of the background tesserae. Cover the surrounding area with a drop cloth because grouting can be messy. Wear rubber gloves to protect your hands and apply the grout using a float or squeegee. Push the grout firmly into the gaps between the tesserae and remove the excess with the squeegee.

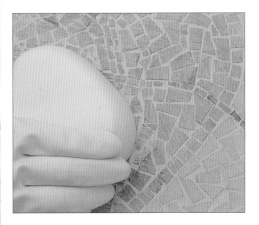

10 Still wearing rubber gloves sponge off the excess grout. Constantly rinse your sponge in clean water, so that you do not smear the surface. Allow to dry, then polish the mosaic using a dry, soft cloth.

INSPIRATIONAL IDEAS

Try this design in different colors. The rich brown urn would look stylish against a sky blue background, while the grapes could be made with green and black tesserae. If you prefer, you could try filling the urn with other varieties of fruit. Blood-red pomegranates were a favorite of the Romans, while lemons and limes are typical Mediterranean fruits.

BEDROOMS & ACCESSORIES

Mirror

TOOLS AND MATERIALS

Vitreous glass tesserae:
³⁄₄ x ³⁄₄in (2 x 2cm)
Sandpaper and block
Surgical and rubber gloves
Pencil and ruler
Wood: 31in (80cm) long x
23in (60cm) wide
Mirror: 23in (60cm) long x
8in (20cm) wide
Gummmed brown paper, or
plain brown paper and gum
Grout float
Craft knife and palette knife
PVA glue and paintbrush
Mosaic nippers
Safety glasses and mask
Powder adhesive and additive
Two buckets for mixing
Margin trowel
Notched trowel: ¹⁄₄in (3mm)
Sponge and cloth
Awl or similar tool
White powder grout
and additive
Blue paint (latex or acrylic)
and paintbrush
Tracing paper

GLASS TESSERAE COLORS

Baby pink
Lilac with gold vein
Candy pink
Blue with gold vein
Mint green with gold vein
Misty white

This elaborate, very feminine mirror has been created from vitreous glass mosaics. The palette is typically Chinese, combining lavish, vibrant colors that challenge the Western eye. The flowers featured are tree peonies, symbolizing Spring, Riches, Honor, Love & Affection, Feminine Beauty, and Prosperity. Similar motifs can be seen in embroidery, textiles, and Chinese ornamental art—painted porcelain vases or bowls and paper-cutting designs, for example. The art of paper cutting, popular during the Ching Ming and earlier dynasties, was obscured by the style adopted during the 19th century, when the utilitarian, practical approach featured prominently and the decorative, more ornate styles were abandoned. It is quite a complicated design, but with patience you'll re-create a beautiful, authentic-looking Chinese mirror that is worth the challenge.

USING THE TEMPLATE

This project involves both the direct and indirect method, explained on pages 10 and 11. You only need to use the template for the two flower borders, where you will follow the indirect method. To do this, trace the template at the back of the book. Turn the tracing paper over and place onto a sheet of brown paper, then draw over the outline of the design on the reverse in pencil. Turn it back over and place it on top of another sheet of brown paper. Trace over the lines once again, transferring the design onto the brown paper. This will produce the flower borders. Then follow the indirect method for laying the tesserae.

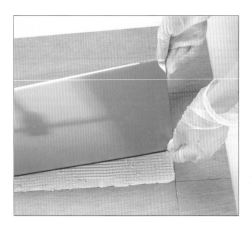

1 Cut the wood to the required dimensions and remove rough edges with sandpaper and a block. Remove the sawdust, then apply a layer of PVA glue with a paintbrush to the front and edges of the wood. Allow to dry.

2 Mark the two borders: bottom and top, 24in (60cm) long x 4in (10cm) wide; the flower panels, 24in (60cm) long x 8in (20cm) wide; and the area where the mirror will be, 24in (60cm) long x 8in (20cm) wide.

3 Mix some adhesive. Apply using a trowel or margin trowel, but stay within the marked outline. Groove the bed using a notched trowel. Position the mirror and push it down firmly into the adhesive with your hands.

5 Trace the flower design onto the brown paper. Then reverse the flower design and trace once again, so you have two panels, both in different directions. See the note about tracing the template on page 66. Cut the mosaic with nippers.

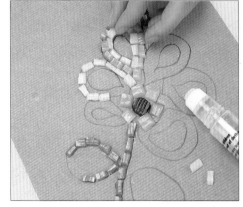

4 Start with the bottom and top borders of the mirror, following the direct method. Using a craft knife, cut a strip of blue mosaics, four tesserae wide, to fit the length. Position these in the adhesive. Line the blue mosaic to the edge of the board. Cut the candy pink mosaic and position it directly into the gap between the blue mosaic and the mirror. Repeat this procedure along the top and bottom of the mirror. Using a damp sponge, wet the paper backing and carefully peel it away from the tesserae.

6 Using a damp sponge on gummed brown paper or gum glue on plain brown paper, stick the tiles into position smooth side down. Complete the detail of the flowers and then the background. Finish both panels.

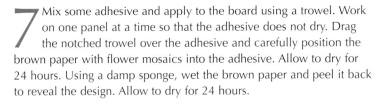

7 Mix some adhesive and apply to the board using a trowel. Work on one panel at a time so that the adhesive does not dry. Drag the notched trowel over the adhesive and carefully position the brown paper with flower mosaics into the adhesive. Allow to dry for 24 hours. Using a damp sponge, wet the brown paper and peel it back to reveal the design. Allow to dry for 24 hours.

8 Prick out any dry excess adhesive, using an awl or similar tool, and clean the surface with a dry cloth. Then mix some white powder grout and apply to the mosaic using a grout float. Clean with a damp sponge and polish. Allow to dry for 24 hours.

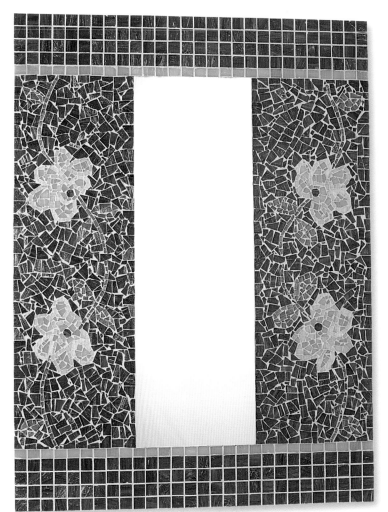

HINTS AND TIPS

▶ Read pages 7, 8, and 9 for guidelines on safety, cutting, and mixing before starting this project.

▶ To free the tesserae from their backing, leave them to soak in warm water, which will dissolve the glue; they will then be ready to use.

▶ Cut brown paper to the exact size needed for the flower borders before sticking on the tesserae. You will need enough brown paper for two borders.

▶ When grouting or using adhesive, fix some newspaper over the mirror with masking tape so that you do not scratch the surface.

▶ When you have finished using the grout float, adhesive trowel, buckets, and paintbrush, wash them immediately.

▶ Paint the back and edges of the mirror with a blue latex or acrylic paint.

▶ To hang the mirror on a wall, attach mirror glass plates to the back of the frame (in the wood) and then screw into the wall. You can buy mirror glass plates from hardware stores.

INSPIRATIONAL IDEAS

This flower border could be repeated around the border of a bathroom floor, or as a baseboard in any other room. Choose complementary colors and remember to use a grout that matches the mosaic.

Japanese Screen

TOOLS AND MATERIALS

Vitreous glass tesserae:
¾ x ¾in (2 x 2cm)
Surgical and rubber gloves
Pencil
Margin trowel and trowel
Awl or similar tool
Grout float
Gummed brown paper, or plain
brown paper and gum glue: 21in
(54cm) long x 11in (28cm) wide
Notched trowel: ¼in (3mm)
Three particle board panels: 72in
(183cm) long x 20in (50cm) wide
x ⅛in (3mm) deep; each panel
should have a rectangle grooved
out: 21in (54cm) long x 11in
(28cm) wide x ⅕in (5mm) deep
Six hinges to attach the panels
Tape measure and tracing paper
PVA glue and paintbrush
Mosaic nippers
Safety glasses and mask
White powder adhesive
and additive
Two buckets for mixing
Palette knife
White powder grout and additive
Drop cloth, sponge, and cloth

GLASS TESSERAE COLORS

Bronze
Shiny black
Charcoal
Jade
Sharp white
Misty white
Brighter white

Screens have always played an important role in the Japanese home, whether they have been designed to divide, conceal, or protect. Traditionally, they are beautifully decorated with recognizable symbols, like the crane featured here, which was inspired by a Japanese screen painted in 1566. Cranes were commonly seen on *objects d'art* and 19th-century textiles. In Japan, cranes symbolize longevity and are also said to aid communication with the Divinities. The whiteness of the crane has been set on a jade green background. Vitreous glass mosaics offer a wide color range, and thus texture and tone can be given to the crane's feathers with the various shades of white tesserae. To finish the screen, it was painted black and varnished to give it a lacquered feel.

USING THE TEMPLATE

Central panel: trace the template at the back of the book, turn over the tracing paper, and draw over the outline on the reverse in pencil. Turn it back over and place it on top of the brown paper. Trace over the front, transferring the design onto the brown paper. First and last panel: a template is not needed for these two panels because they consist of randomly cut pieces of jade mosaic with no pattern.

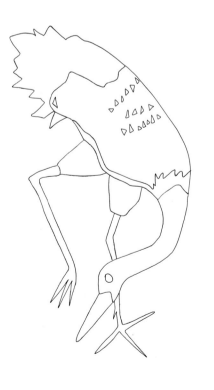

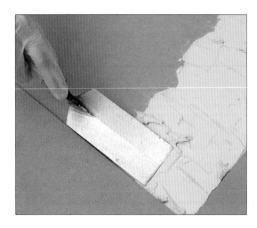

1 Remove any rough edges from the particle board with sandpaper and a block. Then seal with PVA glue. Allow to dry. Wearing rubber gloves, mix some powder adhesive and apply to a portion of one panel with a margin trowel.

2 Groove the surface of the adhesive with a notched trowel. Cut the sage green mosaics in random shapes using mosaic nippers. Stick the tesserae into the adhesive bed, keeping the spaces between them equal. Repeat over first and last panels.

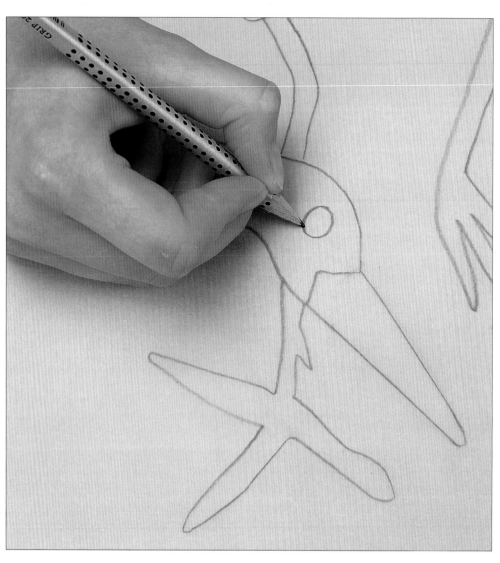

3 Central panel: follow the template instructions as explained on page 70. Trace the design onto some brown paper. It is a good idea to draw over the pencil outline of the crane in black felt-tip pen—this makes it easier to follow when you start sticking down the tiles. Secure the template to your base with masking tape while you are tracing the image, to help keep it in place. Once you have completed the design, cut all the colored tesserae pieces you will need to complete the crane.

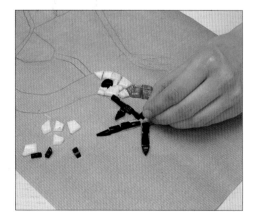

4 Central panel: using a damp sponge on gummed brown paper or gum glue on plain brown paper, stick the tesserae into position smooth side down. Complete the detail of the bird, then the jade background. Allow to dry.

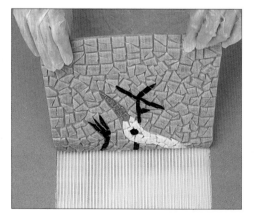

5 Central panel: mix some adhesive and apply it to the central panel, then groove it with the notched trowel. Carefully place the mosaic, paper side up, into the bed of adhesive. Allow it to dry for 24 hours.

6 Central panel: wet the brown paper using a damp sponge and gently peel it away. Make sure you remove all traces of the paper.

▶ Paint the screen with black latex, wait for it to dry, then varnish using clear marine varnish.

▶ A carpenter made the screen featured here. The positioning of the hinges determines the direction or angle of movement of the screen. You must decide how you want it to stand and inform your carpenter.

▶ It is advisable to cut the brown paper to the exact size and shape needed before sticking on the tesserae.

▶ To free the tesserae from their backing, leave them to soak in warm water, which will dissolve the glue; they will then be ready to use.

7 Central, first, and last panels: clean the mosaic with a sponge and prick out any unwanted lumps of adhesive with an awl or similar tool. Work on one panel at a time. Wash the panels with a damp sponge afterwards.

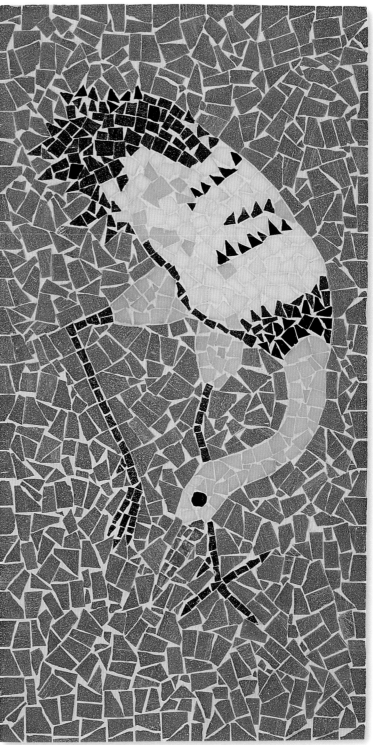

8 Central, first, and last panels: mix some white grout and apply using a grout float. Remove excess grout with a damp sponge and polish with a dry cloth. Work on one panel at a time.

INSPIRATIONAL IDEAS

The bird design could be applied onto some marine plywood, 21in (54cm) long x 11in (28cm) wide, and used as a decorative wall plaque in a garden.

Chinese Photograph Album

T his decorative Chinese photograph album would make an ideal gift or an excellent ornament. The simple color scheme of white, black, and gold creates a stylish look with a touch of wealth. The Chinese symbol used here means "Riches," which could apply to the beautiful handmade album itself as well as the photographs it contains, with all their happy memories. To make the album really special, you could add a leather strap for the tie and place some recycled paper inside, which you can either buy or make yourself. Thick, handmade paper with red rose petals sprinkled on a white background was used here. Rice paper was cut and inserted between each sheet of handmade paper to protect the photographs, which can be attached with adhesive corner mounts.

USING THE TEMPLATE

For Board 2, the front of the album, you should make the circular motif separately on brown paper. Trace the template at the back of the book, turn the tracing paper over, and draw over the outline on the reverse in pencil. Turn it back over and place it on top of brown paper. Trace the lines again, transferring the design onto the brown paper. Once the black border has been laid, you will apply tesserae directly to complete the background—no template is required for this area. For Board 1 (the back of the album), use the template to draw the black border, then apply the tesserae directly onto the rest of the surface.

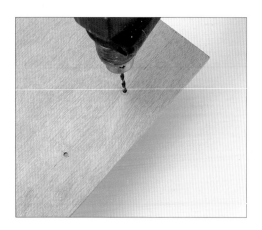

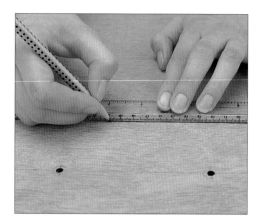

1 Drill two pilot holes through both boards at 2in (5cm) from the width of the board and 4in (10cm) away from the top/length. Remove the rough edges with sandpaper and a block. Then apply PVA glue to the front on the boards. Allow to dry.

2 Paint the back of both boards using black latex paint. Allow to dry, then varnish with clear yacht varnish. Cut the white mosaic in random shapes and the gold leaf in small oblong shapes, but leave the black mosaic on the sheets.

3 On the front of both boards, measure in 4in (10.5cm) from the outside edge. Mark a line at this level, showing where the division between the white and black mosaic should lie.

4 Boards 1 and 2: mix some adhesive and apply it where the black mosaic will be. Groove the surface with a notched trowel, then place the mosaic smooth side up into the adhesive. Remove any tesserae that block the drilled holes.

5 Boards 1 and 2: remove any brown paper from the black tesserae by soaking them in warm water. Cut the mosaic to fit around the holes, making sure that you wear safety glasses when cutting. Place the mosaics into the adhesive.

6 Board 2 (front of album): detach the template from the back of the book, trace the Chinese motif, and transfer the design onto some brown paper (see the instructions on page 74). Using a damp sponge on gummed brown paper or gum glue on plain brown paper, stick the tesserae (the gold leaf and white mosaic) into position smooth side down. Complete the pattern and allow them to dry.

7 Board 2 (front of album): mix some adhesive and apply to the board. Groove the surface of the adhesive with a notched trowel. Position the Chinese motif, paper side up, on top of the adhesive, making sure it is central. Then start sticking the white tesserae, smooth side up, directly into the adhesive. Fit the tesserae together like a jigsaw puzzle. If there are any gaps, you may need to cut exact pieces to fit. Allow to dry for 24 hours. On Board 1 (back of album), position white mosaics into the adhesive, smooth side up. Work around the symbol moving outward until you have reached the edge of the album.

8 Board 2 (front of album): take a damp sponge and wet the paper before peeling back to reveal the motif. Use a bradawl to prick out any unwanted adhesive.

9 Mix some grout and apply it to Boards 1 and 2 using a grout float. Remove excess grout with a damp sponge and polish. Allow to dry for 24 hours.

INSPIRATIONAL IDEAS

This motif has such a beautiful appearance and meaning that it would make a wonderful wall plaque or a picture. You could find other Chinese symbols that appeal to you and create other mosaic projects.

HINTS AND TIPS

▶ It is advisable to cut the brown paper to the exact size and shape needed before sticking on the tesserae.

▶ To free the tesserae from their backing, leave them to soak in warm water, which will dissolve the glue; they will then be ready to use.

▶ Always read the advice given on cutting, safety, and mixing on pages 7, 8, and 9.

▶ After using PVA glue, wash your paintbrush immediately with soapy water.

▶ Remove excess varnish from your paintbrush following the instructions given by manufacturer.

▶ You will need to cut the handmade and rice paper sheets to size and punch holes in them in the correct positions to match the outer shell of the album.

Plum Blossom Headboard

TOOLS AND MATERIALS

Vitreous glass tesserae:
¾ x ¾in (2 x 2cm)
Fine black pen
Electric drill and countersink bit
Sandpaper and block
Surgical and rubber gloves
Awl or similar tool
Palette knife
Grout float
Circle of wood: 8in (21cm) radius,
16in (42cm) diameter
Ten screws: 1in (2.5cm)
Two pieces of wood: long enough
to span the width of the bed,
wide enough to reach from floor
to just above pillows
Mosaic nippers
Safety glasses and mask
Notched trowel: ¼in (3mm)
Two buckets for mixing
Powder adhesive and additive
Trowel
Sponge
Cloth
PVA glue and paintbrush
White powder grout and additive
Tracing paper and pencil
White gloss paint and paintbrush
Mineral spirits

VITREOUS GLASS MOSAICS

Bright white
Bronze
Pink with gold vein
Lilac with gold vein
Mint green with gold vein
Candy pink

Futon beds have become popular accessories in the modern home. To update your futon, why not make a unique piece of artwork—a decorative headboard. The mosaic features plum blossoms representing the return of spring. This design was inspired by an antique Chinese woman's informal robe, known as "pei," with plum blossoms adorned on the front, back, sleeves, and hem. The colors of the glass mosaic tiles are pretty pinks and purples that have gold veins running through them, similar to the colored silks and threads seen in traditional Chinese robes and embroidery. The petals, which are a major feature in the design, are made from glass tesserae cut into circles. The branch of the plum blossoms is made by cutting tesserae in half, then quarters, then eighths, to create small tesserae for outlining.

USING THE TEMPLATE

Trace the template at the back of the book, turn the tracing paper over, and draw over the outline of the plum blossoms on the reverse in pencil. Turn it back over and center it on the board. Trace over the front, transferring the design onto the board. If the lines are too faint, draw over them with a fine black pen.

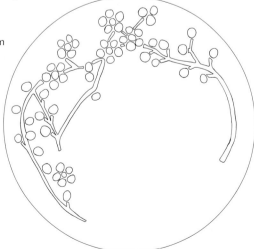

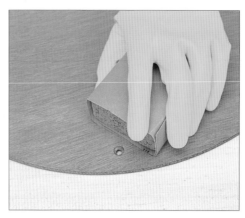

1 Drill pilot holes through the top and bottom of the wood circle, ¾in (2cm) in from the edge. Drill through the holes with a countersink bit, which will hide the screwheads.

2 Using sandpaper and a block, remove the rough edges around the circle and the drilled holes, then apply PVA glue to the wood with a paintbrush. Sand the two remaining pieces of wood and paint them with white gloss paint.

3 Detach the template from the back of the book and trace the design. Then transfer the design from the tracing paper onto the circle of wood. See page 78 for full instructions on using the template.

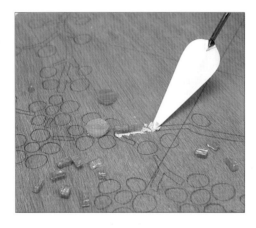

4 Cut the mosaic tiles. Apply a small amount of adhesive and position each tile, working on the details first. The flowers are made from cut circles, and the branches are made by cutting the tesserae into eighths (see page 8 for instructions).

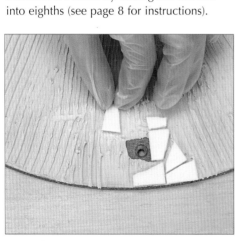

5 Once all the details are completed, start on the background, which is made of randomly cut white mosaic. Make sure the drilled holes are not covered with adhesive.

6 Prick out the excess cement using an awl or similar tool. Wipe the mosaic surface clean with a damp sponge. Once the mosaic is complete, allow it to dry for 24 hours. Make sure that you reserve some white mosaic pieces to cover over the drilled holes.

7 Mix some white powder grout to a smooth consistency, then apply it to the surface of the mosaic using the grout float. Wear rubber gloves to protect your hands when grouting. Wipe off the excess grout and polish the surface with a dry cloth. Allow the mosaic to dry for 24 hours.

8 Screw the two painted pieces of wood to the wall. Center the circle between them, and make a pencil mark through each of the drilled holes. Remove the circle and drill two holes through the marks. Put the mosaic back into position and insert the screws. You may need a friend to help you hold the mosaic while you screw it into position. Mix some adhesive and stick the few remaining tesserae over the screwheads. Let it dry for 24 hours, then grout, clean, and polish.

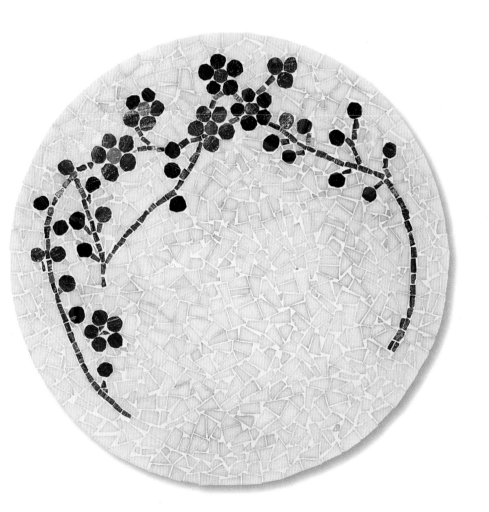

HINTS AND TIPS

▶ To free the tesserae from their backing, leave them to soak in warm water, which will dissolve the glue; they will then be ready to use.

▶ Always read the safety tips and cutting and grouting advice given on pages 7, 8, and 9 before you begin a project.

▶ While working on the mosaic, if you get any adhesive onto the tesserae, wipe them clean with a damp sponge.

▶ Wear surgical gloves when applying cement-based adhesive.

▶ Wear rubber gloves when applying grout.

▶ Wash your paintbrush with liquid detergent immediately after using PVA glue.

▶ Remove white gloss paint from your paintbrush immediately with mineral spirits.

INSPIRATIONAL IDEAS

If you want a soft headboard, cover the two painted pieces of wood with some batting, cover with fabric, and staple the fabric in place. This would be easier to do before you attach the wood to the wall. Or you could use this design as a decorative wall hanging instead of a headboard.

Gilded Minaret Mirror

T his exquisite mirror combines a bold architectural outline with a delicate and intricate design. The result is an authentic-looking product of North Africa. The undulating design is reminiscent of Arabic script, but with an organic essence, as it twists and twines its way around the frame. Although this is one of the more complicated projects in the book, it is relatively easy once you get started, so do not be afraid to take on the challenge. Once you have mastered the scoring and snapping of the tiles, it will be plain sailing. Whether resting on a mantelpiece in bright sunshine or illuminated by candles at night, this mirror, with its midnight blue and gold leaf glass, will conjure up the atmosphere, magic, and mystery of the Arabian Nights.

TOOLS AND MATERIALS

Two pieces of particle board: 2ft (60cm) long x 11in (28cm) wide x ½in (1cm) deep
Pencil and ruler
Jigsaw
Tracing paper
Electric drill
PVA glue
Paintbrush
C-clamps or heavy weights
Tesserae: ¼ x ¾in (2 x 2cm); two sheets of blue glass and 100 gold leaf tesserae
Mosaic nippers
Tile cutters
Surgical and rubber gloves
Safety glasses and mask
Two buckets for mixing
Gray powder adhesive and additive
Trowel
Fine paintbrush
Sandpaper and block
Awl or similar tool
Gray powder grout and additive
Squeegee
Sponge
Cloth
Mirror: 1½ft x 7½in (47 x 19cm)
Hardboard: 1½ft x 7½in (47 x 19cm)
Finish nails and hammer

TESSERAE COLORS

Midnight blue with gold fleck
Gold leaf

USING THE TEMPLATE

Trace the template at the back of the book, turn the tracing paper over, and draw over the outline on the reverse in pencil. Turn the tracing back over and place it on the first piece of particle board. Trace the border design over the front, transferring the design onto the particle board. Lift the tracing off and place it on the second piece of particle board and repeat, tracing the minaret shape.

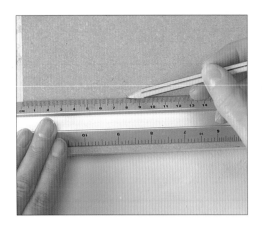

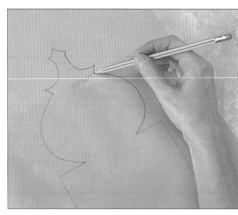

HINTS AND TIPS

▶ When tracing the curly pattern onto the mirror frame, you may need to draw over the outline again because the PVA glue is a difficult surface to mark with pencil.

▶ If the adhesive outline dries before you get a chance to cover it with gold tesserae, simply rub it off with sandpaper and start the outline again.

▶ Set yourself a small section to complete at a time—do not try to mosaic too much in one go; it will probably take a few sittings to finish.

▶ To attach the mirror into the frame, first paint the back of the frame black, paying special attention to the edges of the minaret. Slot in the mirror and hardboard backing. Then secure with nails, gently hammering them into the side of the frame so that they prevent the mirror and backing from falling out.

1 To make the mirror frame, take one piece of particle board and measure 1½in (4cm) in from the bottom and sides. Make several marks along these edges. Along the top, measure in 2in (8cm) and make marks. Join up all the marks to form a rectangle. Use a jigsaw to cut out this shape.

2 Using the template at the back of the book, trace the outline of the minaret onto the second piece of wood. Be sure to center the design. Remember to use a soft pencil for the reverse tracing as it will maximize the carbon on the back and give a stronger traced line.

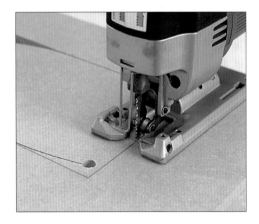

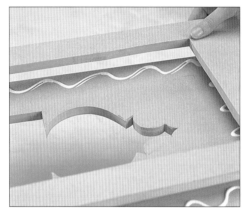

3 Drill a hole in the second piece of particle board, insert the jigsaw, and cut out the minaret. Cut the straight lines first, then guide the jigsaw gently around the curves. You may have to drill extra holes to get into tight corners. Do not push the jigsaw to speed up this part of the process—the particle board will cut easily if you let the jigsaw proceed at its own pace.

4 Squeeze a good quantity of strong PVA glue onto the back of the second piece of particle board (the minaret shape), keeping within the confines of the border. Clamp the two pieces of particle board together, or position a heavy object on top, and allow to dry. With a paintbrush, apply a layer of PVA glue as a sealant. Allow to dry until the glue is transparent.

5 Using mosaic nippers, cut the blue glass tiles into halves and then quarters. You will need these for the inside edge of the mirror. It doesn't matter if the shapes are irregular or if the tiles shatter. This design can accommodate a variety of irregular shapes. Cut lots of small triangles at different angles. Keep all the bits that splinter off as they will always find a home somewhere.

6 Score and snap the gold leaf tesserae with tile cutters, using the method described on page 8. To make tiny triangles, score the tesserae from corner to corner and then snap. Insert only around a quarter of the tesserae into the cutters, using the scored line as a central guide. Apply gentle pressure and the tesserae should snap easily, with minimal shattering. Continue dividing the triangles until they are small enough. For the tiny rectangles, divide the tiles in half before scoring and snapping. Use the nippers to create little pieces. You should be able to get four small pieces from one half.

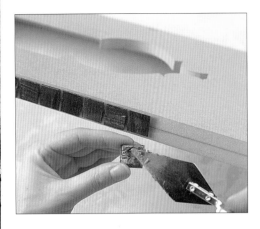

7 Mix a small quantity of adhesive (see page 9). Starting on the outside edge, apply adhesive to whole tiles and hold each one in position for a couple of seconds. Work your way around the whole frame. If, when you are nearing an edge, it becomes clear that a gap is too small for a whole tile, add a half tile somewhere along the line.

8 Using either halves or quarters, move on to the inside edge of the minaret. The straight edges are easy and the curves are slightly trickier. Apply adhesive to each mosaic piece as before and hold in place. Allow to dry for at least three hours before starting the main design.

9 Trace the curly pattern onto the mirror frame. Mix a quantity of runny adhesive and use a fine paintbrush to apply it to the tracing. Do this in lines and work quickly before it dries. If you are too optimistic and the adhesive dries before you get there, sand it off and start again.

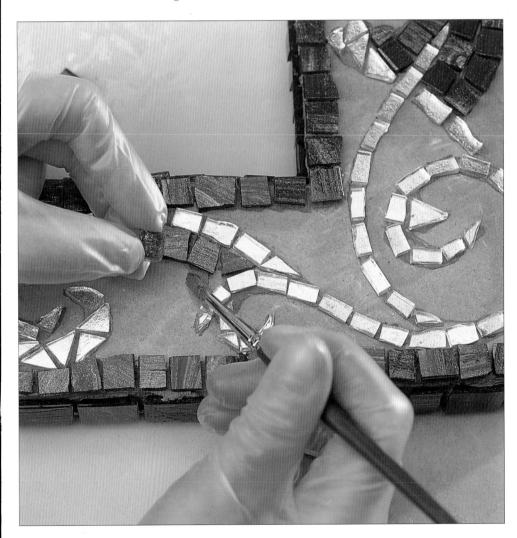

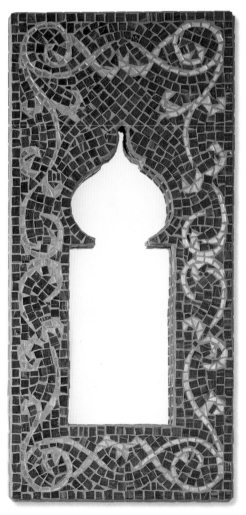

10 Fill in the background with quarter blue tiles, working in lines against the gold curves to give them the illusion of movement. You will need a lot of irregular pieces and triangles to fill in all the gaps. Allow to dry for 24 hours before pricking out the excess adhesive with an awl or similar tool. Mix some grout (see page 9) and spread it over the design with a squeegee, pushing it into the gaps. Wipe away excess with a damp sponge. Allow to dry for 24 hours and polish with a cloth. See *Hints and Tips* for hanging the mirror.

INSPIRATIONAL IDEAS

For a glamorous interior, the curly gold design could be used as a baseboard and continued around the door casing.

GARDENS & OUTDOOR AREAS

Wall Tiles

Create a Zen feel in your garden by adding these simple, yet stylish, garden tiles to any wall. Their refined design is a great backdrop for relaxation and calm. In the Chinese and Japanese school of Mahayana Buddhism, it is believed that enlightenment can be attained through the practice of reflection and meditation. Add the tiles to a peaceful corner of your garden to complement a relaxed seating area with a screen of Asian bamboo. This is an ideal first project for beginners as there is no cutting involved. The color scheme used here features marble mosaics in black, cream, green, terra-cotta, and white with gray flecks. The marble has been polished to add to the elegant look. Feel free to experiment and create your own tiles by using different mosaic colors or a different design.

TOOLS AND MATERIALS

Polished marble tesserae:
⅝ x ⅝in (1.5 x 1.5cm)
PVA glue and paintbrush
Surgical and rubber gloves
Scissors
Awl or similar tool
Six pieces of marine plywood:
8in (20cm) long x 8hn (20cm)
wide x ¾in (2cm) deep
Sponge
White powder grout
and additive
Notched trowel: ¼in (3mm)
Trowel
Cloth
Safety glasses and mask
Marble protector
Color enhancer
Marble impregnator
Craft knife
Sandpaper and block
White powder adhesive
and additive
Two buckets for mixing
Grout float
Paintbrush and white latex
(or a color of your choice)
Tracing paper and pencil
Clear marine varnish

MARBLE TESSERAE COLORS

Black
White with gray flecks
Green
Terra-cotta
Cream

USING THE TEMPLATE

Trace the template at the back of the book, turn the tracing paper over, and draw over the outline on the reverse in pencil. Turn it back over and place it on top of the marine plywood. Trace over the front, transferring the design onto the board, ready to use the direct method as explained on page 10. There are four separate designs and two plain designs that do not need a template.

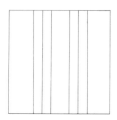
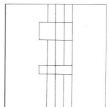
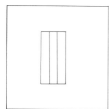
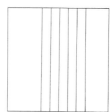

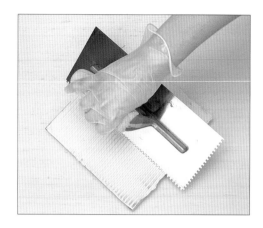

1 Remove the rough edges from all six pieces of plywood, using sandpaper and a block. Clean away the dust with a dry cloth. Apply a coat of PVA glue to the top and edges of the board and allow it to dry.

2 Leave the mosaics on the plastic or paper backing on which they are supplied and cut the sheet with scissors. Trace the template at the back of the book and place the tesserae into position on the tracing, one wall tile at a time.

3 Mix some adhesive and apply it onto the wood with a trowel; smooth down. Then drag the notched trowel back toward you at a 45° angle, making grooves. The grooves will provide a good tooth into which the tesserae can bond.

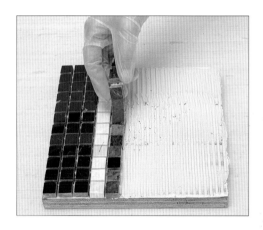

4 Transfer the marble line by line into the adhesive. Work on one tile at a time so that the adhesive doesn't dry out. You may need to use a ruler to keep the mosaic running in straight lines.

5 Once all six tiles are completed, allow them to dry for 24 hours. Clean with a damp sponge and remove excess adhesive with an awl or similar tool.

6 Apply a marble impregnator and protector with a clean paintbrush (read the manufacturer's instructions for drying time). Mix enough white powder grout for six tiles and apply using the grout float. Push the grout firmly into the spaces between the tesserae. Wipe away the excess grout with a damp sponge. Allow to dry for 24 hours.

7 Clean the tiles with a dry cloth to remove grout residue. Once the grout has dried, paint the edges and backs of the tiles a color of your choice (white was used for our tiles). Then varnish them for extra protection against all weather conditions.

8 Apply a marble color enhancer with a cloth and allow to dry. As the name suggests, this will bring out the color of the marble and protect it. If you have any queries, it is best to seek advice from your marble supplier.

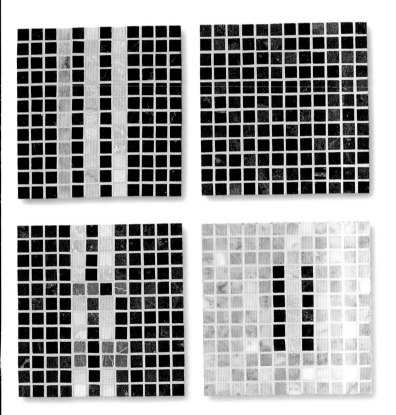

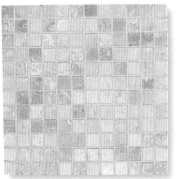

HINTS AND TIPS

▶ If you are experimenting with different mosaic colors or designs, make sure the type of mosaic you choose is suitable for exterior use and that the board is the correct size to fit all the tiles.

▶ Ask advice from a hardware store about the best method of attaching the tiles to the garden wall.

▶ Wash your paintbrush immediately after use to remove any PVA glue. Also wash adhesive and grouting tools after use.

▶ Apply PVA glue to the edges of the marine plywood because, although the wood is waterproof, any cut edges are not.

▶ Work on one tile at a time until you reach the grouting stage, which can be completed in one go.

▶ Before grouting, it is helpful to brush on a marble impregnator followed by a marble protector, available from most tile suppliers. These protect the marble from dirt and staining.

▶ Remove any adhesive that seeps over the side with a damp sponge.

▶ Read pages 7, 8, and 9 for advice on safety and mixing before starting this project.

INSPIRATIONAL IDEAS

These tiles could also be used as indoor wall hangings. You do not need to make all six. You could repeat the design and turn it into a beautiful floor pattern or kitchen backsplash—obviously, you would not need wood for this. They could also be made into tablemats and you could produce smaller versions for cups and glasses.

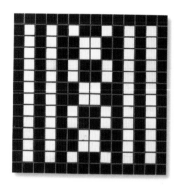

Garden Stepping Stones

TOOLS AND MATERIALS

Ceramic tesserae:
³/₄ x ³/₄in (18 x 18mm)
Concrete pavers:
12 x 12in (30 x 30cm)
Gummed brown paper, or plain
brown paper and gum glue
Tracing paper and pencil
Craft knife
PVA glue
Fine paintbrush
Sponge
Concrete sealer and brush
Two buckets for mixing
Gray exterior powder adhesive
Grey exterior powder grout
Surgical gloves and rubber gloves
Safety glasses and mask
Tile cutters
Mosaic nippers
Trowel
Notched trowel: ¼in (3mm)
Cloth

CERAMIC TESSERAE COLORS

Dark blue
Black
White

This is a simple yet effective project that does not take long to complete. It is extremely satisfying to make because it looks deceptively complex. The stones are decorated with three geometric designs that are translated into six different patterns by reversing the color schemes. There is some cutting involved, but the pieces do not have to be perfectly even so it is not difficult. Muted tones of dusky blue, black, and chalky white are used to create a harmonious classical effect. In some villages on the Greek islands, these patterns are used to decorate the outside of houses. The islanders mix and match a variety of designs but with a very limited palette, sometimes only two colors, to create greater impact. Despite the antiquity of the designs, the finished result looks stylish and modern.

USING THE TEMPLATE

Trace the template at the back of the book. Note that the designs on the template only show half of each pattern. Turn the tracing paper over and draw over the outline on the reverse in pencil. Turn the tracing back over and position it on the brown paper. Trace over the front, transferring a copy of each half design onto the brown paper. Then turn the template over and trace each design again. Each paver requires two halves of the design, so you will have to match up the two halves to make the complete pattern for each stone.

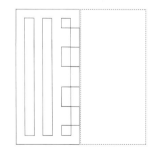 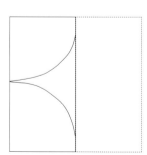 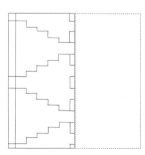

1 Seal all the pavers with a concrete sealer. This is usually white when you apply it and gets clearer when it is dry, like PVA. Choose the flattest pavers you can, but if they are a bit uneven, you can even them out when you apply the adhesive.

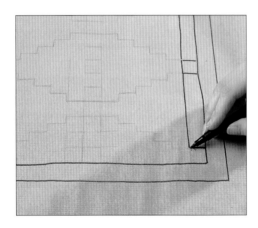

2 Trace two copies of each design onto pieces of brown paper. The template only shows half of the pattern; to create the whole pattern for each paver, trace the template once, then turn it over and trace again, two halves for each paver.

3 Using a damp sponge on gummed brown paper or gum glue on plain brown paper, stick the whole tiles into position smooth side down. Score and snap rectangles to fill in the sections that are too small to fit whole tiles on the star-patterned stone. Make the shapes you need by holding the tesserae and cutting them a third of the way down at an angle so that you get irregular pieces. Make sure you follow the advice on cutting given on page 8.

4 When all the tiles are stuck down, trim the edges of the brown paper with a craft knife. This makes it easier to position the tiles on the pavers and ensure that the mosaic is aligned at the edges.

5 Cover the pavers with adhesive using a notched trowel and gently lower each piece of paper onto them, tile side down. Push the design gently into the adhesive, making sure they are embedded well enough to stick.

HINTS AND TIPS

▶ If the pavers are chipped, it is a good idea to level them out with a bit of adhesive and allow this to dry completely before you get to step 5 in the project.

▶ The grout might not get into all the gaps and holes may appear while you are working; if so, simply rub grout into the holes to fill them up.

▶ When you are pressing the tesserae on their brown paper backing into the adhesive, remember that you are not trying to fill in the gaps between the tesserae, but make sure the tiles are embedded well enough in the adhesive for them to stick.

▶ Clean any tools used for applying adhesive and grout immediately after use.

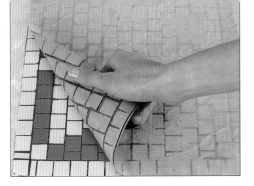  

6 Allow the pavers to dry overnight. Dampen the paper with water and wait for it to come loose. Gently peel back each piece till all six patterns are revealed. Stick down any tesserae that come loose.

7 Using an awl or similar tool, prick out any adhesive that has squeezed its way through to the surface and dust away the powder. Be meticulous, because the adhesive and grout might vary in color and will be visible later if left in place.

8 Mix up enough grout for all the tiles and trowel it into the gaps. The edges of the pavers may be uneven or a different color, so for a more professional look, you should grout the edges of the tiles.

9 Wipe off any excess grout and polish the tiles to reveal the true colors of the tesserae. All that remains is to lower the pavers into the positions you want them in your garden.

INSPIRATIONAL IDEAS

Try changing the colors used for this design to earth tones—rich terra-cottas and warm ochers—to give a rustic feel. You could use half of the template and repeat it to create an attractive edging border rather than turning it over to create a square. Or use one design repeated over and over to create a border or stripe down a garden path.

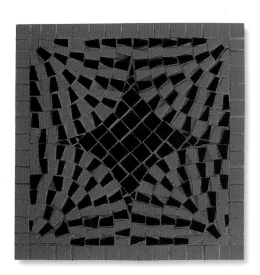 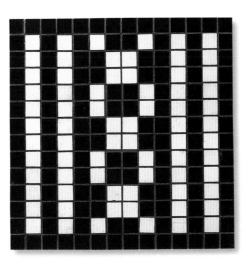 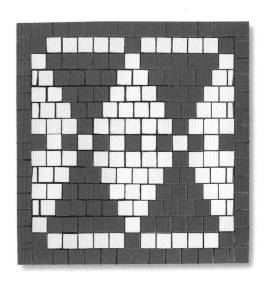

Seahorse Wall Frieze

TOOLS AND MATERIALS

Glass tesserae: ¾ x ¾in (2 x 2cm)
Tracing paper and pencil
Masking tape
Waterproof PVA glue
Paintbrush
Level
Tape measure
Awl or similar tool
White exterior powder adhesive
White exterior powder grout
Safety glasses and mask
Two buckets for mixing
Trowel
Sponge and cloth
Mosaic nippers
Surgical and rubber gloves

GLASS TESSERAE COLORS

Sea green
Pale aqua
Dark sea green
Leaf green
Grass green

Greek mythology is steeped in fantastic stories about sea creatures, and they are replicated in many classical mosaics. Tiny seahorses are among the most charming marine animals, and this project combines waves of seahorses with an interlinking chain design. The chain is traditionally used in Greek art and architecture, as part of a larger design, to create a border or just in its own right. This project is simpler than it may at first appear. The majority of the tesserae are whole or just have their edges nipped off. The only real cutting and detail is in the seahorses. The tesserae are applied using the direct method (see page 10). This versatile design would look stunning in the garden, as we have used it here, or running around a bathroom wall as a chair rail border.

USING THE TEMPLATE

Trace the template at the back of the book, turn the tracing paper over, and draw over the outline on the reverse in pencil. Turn the tracing back over and position it on the wall. Trace over the front, transferring the design onto the wall. You may wish to draw over this outline again with a marker pen to make sure it is clearly visible when you come to stick down the tesserae. Repeat the tracing to fill the length of wall that you want the frieze to run along.

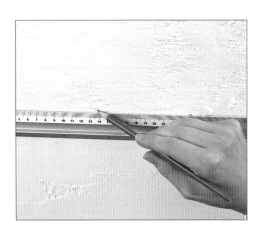

1 Draw parallel lines in pencil on the wall in the position where you want the frieze to run, 12in (30.5cm) apart. Use a tape measure and level to ensure that the lines are straight.

2 Stick masking tape along the top edge of the top line and along the bottom of the bottom line. These are the guidelines for the whole project and will make sticking and grouting much easier.

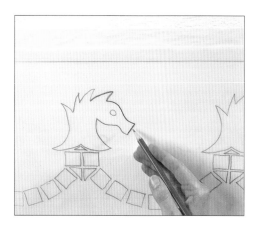

3 Choose the direction you want the seahorses to face and trace the design onto the wall. You may want to draw over the lines freehand with a marker pen so you can see them better.

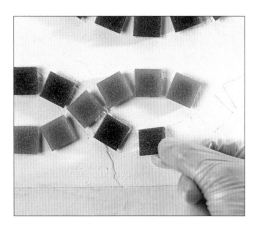

4 Start with the lines between the seahorses and the linking chains, which only use whole tiles. Mix up white adhesive and spread it on each tessera, then press them down one by one.

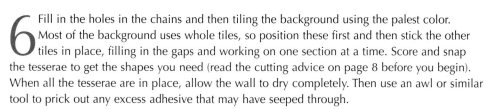

5 Cut heaps of half tiles, quarters, triangles, and little rectangles to work on the seahorses. Cut the eye shapes by nibbling a quarter tile into a circular shape. Work your way from the nose up the head and then down from the mane to the neck.

6 Fill in the holes in the chains and then tiling the background using the palest color. Most of the background uses whole tiles, so position these first and then stick the other tiles in place, filling in the gaps and working on one section at a time. Score and snap the tesserae to get the shapes you need (read the cutting advice on page 8 before you begin). When all the tesserae are in place, allow the wall to dry completely. Then use an awl or similar tool to prick out any excess adhesive that may have seeped through.

7 Mix the grout and cover the whole surface between the masking tape guidelines. The grout needs to be fairly solid so that it does not slide down the walls.

8 Wipe off the excess grout with a cloth and polish the mosaic to bring out the true colors. Peel off the masking tape from above and below, and the frieze is complete.

INSPIRATIONAL IDEAS

You could use this linking border around anything. Try it surrounding a garden water feature, such as a fountain or fish pond. For a really authentic Greek appearance, you could have white seahorses with a Mediterranean blue background, which looks simple yet striking. Or use metallic tesserae to make the pattern glisten.

HINTS AND TIPS

▶ For the seahorses' manes, cut whole tesserae into halves and then cut them again diagonally to create triangles.

▶ If the masking tape gets covered in adhesive, peel it off and replace it to make a neater edge when grouting.

▶ You may need to touch up the edges with paint, so it would be useful if you have some left over from when you last painted the wall.

Dolphin Water Feature

The Romans loved water and bathing, and nearly all Roman villas contained a fountain or water feature of some kind. In this modern fountain, water flows from between the two dolphins' heads, almost as though it is coming from their mouths. These playful creatures are a popular motif and can be found all over the Roman world—a similar wall mosaic was created in Carthage, North Africa, in the 4th century B.C. Rather than using the more traditional marble, this mosaic is made from porcelain tesserae, which come in a wide variety of colors and tones that are well-suited to the Roman palette. Porcelain is also frostproof, which makes it ideal for use in a garden or sunroom. For a water feature of this kind, a pump should be installed with a reservoir beneath ground level.

USING THE TEMPLATE

Trace the template at the back of the book, turn the tracing paper over, and draw over the outline of the dolphin on the reverse in pencil. Turn it back over and place it over one half of the board. Trace over the outline on the front, transferring the design onto the board. Then turn the dolphin template over to the other half of the board, so that the image is reversed, and trace the second dolphin. You should end up with two dolphins facing each other.

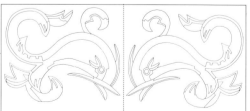

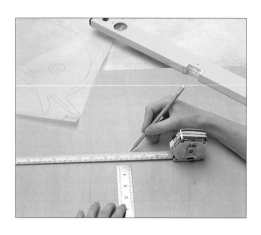

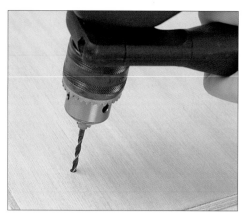

1 Use a level and pencil to draw a center line along the board, from top to bottom. With the aid of a tape measure, make three marks along the board 2¾in (7cm) from the top. Join the marks to make a border line. Repeat 2in (5cm) from the bottom.

2 Drill screw holes for attaching the mosaic to the wall later. For a board that is 4ft (1.2m) long x 2ft (60cm) wide, drill six holes—three along the top and bottom edges.

3 Now drill through the holes with a countersink bit. This will produce a halo or circle around the edge of the hole, which will prevent the screwhead from protruding. Remove any rough edges with sandpaper and a block.

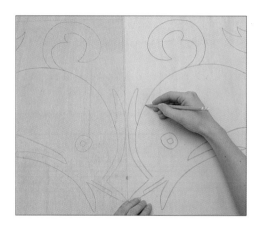

4 Trace the template (see *Using the Template*) so that you have two dolphins facing each other. Drill a hole for the water to come through in the space between the dolphins' noses. Coat the edges of the board with PVA glue using a paintbrush.

5 Cut the tesserae with mosaic nippers. Use quarters on the body and background, and smaller pieces on the tail, nose, and eye. Mix up some adhesive and trowel it onto small sections at a time. Use tweezers to position smaller pieces.

6 Complete the dolphins' bodies before moving onto the background. Make a halo around the dolphins using quarters of white tesserae. Work across the board, filling in the background. Finally, fill in the border and allow to dry for 24 hours. The drilled holes must be kept free of adhesive and tesserae. When dry, use an awl or similar tool to prick the mosaic free of any excess adhesive. Mix some white grout, and using a float, spread grout over the mosaic. Clean, polish, and allow to dry for 24 hours. Apply a porcelain sealant.

7 Coat the battens with marine varnish to protect them. You will need a friend to help you with the rest of this step and the next. Hold the mosaic against the wall where you want it to hang. Make sure it is straight by using a level. Draw lines to mark the top, bottom and sides of the mosaic position. Hold the first batten against the wall. The top should align with the top of the mosaic and it should not overlap the sides. Drill holes through the batten into the wall. Take the batten away and insert plastic wall anchors into the holes, then position the batten and fix. Use screws that are long enough to go through the batten and into the wall. Repeat with the second batten.

8 To attach the mosaic in place, position it on the battens. Ask a friend to help you hold the mosaic while you screw it to the battens. Once the screws are in place, mix some adhesive and stick the remaining tesserae onto the adhesive. Allow 24 hours to dry, then grout, clean, and polish.

HINTS AND TIPS

To create a water feature, dig a hole in the ground to make a reservoir in which the water can be collected—use a large bucket with a metal grate over the top. Pumps are available from garden centers. Full installation instructions will be provided, but you should seek advice from an electrician.

To change the size of the design, create a grid over the original design by drawing vertical and horizontal lines that are equally spaced. You can draw the next step directly onto the desired surface, but if you are likely to want to use the new design again, it is best to draw it onto paper or tracing paper first and then use that as a template. Draw an enlarged or decreased grid onto your surface or piece of paper. The grid must contain exactly the same number of squares, but the lines should be closer together or farther apart, depending on whether you are reducing or enlarging the image. Look at each individual square of the original design and transfer exactly what you see into the corresponding square on the new design. Alternately, you could resize the design on a photocopier.

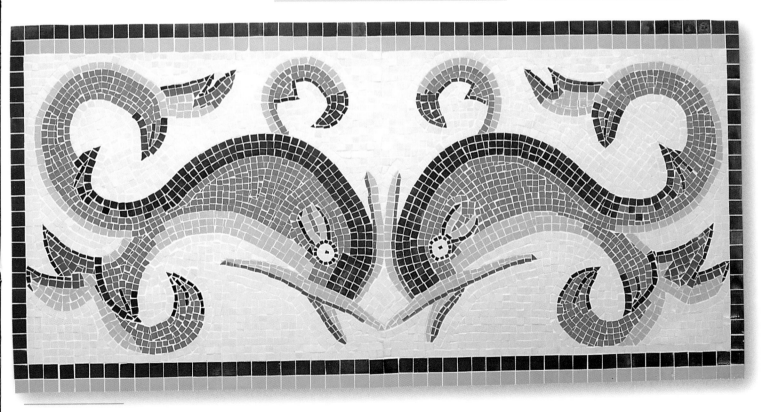

INSPIRATIONAL IDEAS

One or both of these dolphins would make an ideal backsplash for a bathroom or could be used to decorate a shower or garden pond. Experiment with different color schemes and materials—blue and gold vitreous glass would work especially well with water.

Roman Knot Paver

TOOLS AND MATERIALS

Tracing paper
Pencil
Gummed brown paper, or plain
brown paper and gum glue
Cinca porcelain tesserae:
1 x 1in (2.5 x 2.5cm)
Metal ruler
Mosaic nippers
Paintbrush
PVA waterproof exterior glue
Margin trowel
Surgical and rubber gloves
Safety glasses and mask
Pavers with flat, smooth faces:
1⅓ x 1⅓ft (40 x 40cm)
Notched trowel: ¼in (3mm)
Adhesive and additive
Two buckets for mixing
Sponge
Awl or similar tool
White and gray powder grout
and additive
Grout float
Cloth
Porcelain sealant

PORCELAIN TESSERAE COLORS

White
Terra-cotta
Black

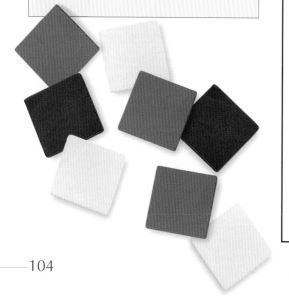

Decorate your garden with these eye-catching mosaic pavers. Whether you arrange them in a group to create a focal point, or spread them out to make a path of stepping stones, they will bring color and interest to the garden through all the seasons. This ancient design, known as "Solomon's Knot," was extremely popular in Roman times, and often featured in floor mosaics. The twists and turns of the stylish knot pattern will serve as an elegant feature in any garden. This mosaic employs a typically Roman palette of terra-cotta, black, and white. Porcelain mosaics have been chosen because they are frostproof and ideal for exterior use. The indirect mosaic-laying method (see page 11) is ideal for this project.

USING THE TEMPLATE

Trace the template at the back of the book. Turn your tracing paper over and draw over the outline of the design on the reverse in pencil. Turn it back over and place it on top of some brown paper. Trace over the lines once again, transferring the design onto the brown paper. Then follow the indirect method (see page 11) for laying the tesserae.

1 Trace the knot template at the back of the book and transfer it onto some brown paper. Make sure the paper has been cut to the size of the paver—in this example, 1⅓ x 1⅓ft (40 x 40cm).

2 Using a damp sponge on gummed brown paper or gum glue on plain brown paper, stick the black tesserae smooth side down around the edge to create a border. Line up the tesserae against a metal ruler to make sure they are straight.

3 Cut the terra-cotta and white mosaics into quarters using mosaic nippers (see page 8). Stick them onto the brown paper, starting from the center of the knot and working outward. Once the knot detail is complete, start on the edges using the white tesserae. Some of these will need to be cut into specific shapes to fit around the twists and turns of the design. To do this, hold the tesserae over the space, draw where the cut needs to be, and then cut. Allow the mosaic to dry for 24 hours.

4 Apply PVA glue with a paintbrush to the smooth upper side of the paver. Wear surgical gloves and wash the brush immediately after use.

5 Mix the adhesive and additive, and wearing surgical gloves, apply with a trowel. A margin trowel, which has a square head, is ideal for covering square areas. It is best to put the adhesive into the center, then spread and work it outward.

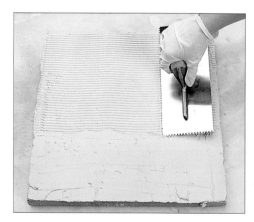

6 Once the paver has been covered with adhesive, use the trowel to smooth it down. Holding the notched trowel at a 45° angle, drag it toward you across the surface of the adhesive. Repeat this action over the entire paver.

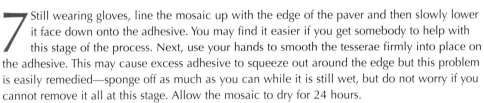

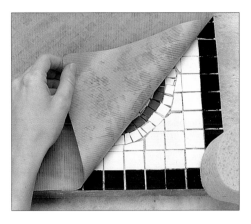

8 Gently wipe a damp sponge over the brown paper, which should start to come away from the surface. Peel back the paper to reveal the knot mosaic design underneath. Wash away any residue that is left behind.

7 Still wearing gloves, line the mosaic up with the edge of the paver and then slowly lower it face down onto the adhesive. You may find it easier if you get somebody to help with this stage of the process. Next, use your hands to smooth the tesserae firmly into place on the adhesive. This may cause excess adhesive to squeeze out around the edge but this problem is easily remedied—sponge off as much as you can while it is still wet, but do not worry if you cannot remove it all at this stage. Allow the mosaic to dry for 24 hours.

9 Use an awl or similar tool to prick out any unwanted adhesive that may be attached to the tesserae. If it is showing through the gaps, it will still show even after the tiles have been grouted. Clean with a damp sponge.

10 Mix the grout in the ratio of 3 parts white to 1 part gray. Wearing rubber gloves, put some grout in the center and use a float to spread it into the corners. Once the paver is covered, remove any excess grout with the float.

11 Clean the mosaic with a damp sponge, then dry and polish with a cloth. Allow to dry for 24 hours. Once all the grime and dirt is removed, use a porcelain protector to seal the mosaic. Allow to dry and install in your garden.

INSPIRATIONAL IDEAS

This versatile design could be used on a wall

or a piece of furniture, such as a table.

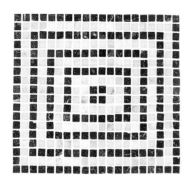

Geometric-patterned Table

This simple but stunning tabletop is an ideal mosaic project for beginners. It can be made from whole mosaic tesserae, so no cutting is involved. The design is inspired by Roman geometric patterns that were often used for decorating paving—the Romans used grids, rulers, and compasses to ensure perfect symmetry. Re-creating this project is incredibly easy. Arrange the marble tesserae on the template and then transfer them in rows to a wooden base that has been covered with adhesive. A white powder grout sets off the design. The table base used here was specially commissioned and carefully planned so that the mosaic would fit perfectly. The table has a black metal base to complement the black and white marble mosaic, and is made from galvanized steel so that the table can be used outside.

TOOLS AND MATERIALS

Unpolished marble tesserae:
⅝ x ⅝in (1.5 x 1.5cm)
Craft knife
Marine plywood: x 2ft (60cm)
long x 1⅓ft (40.5cm) wide x
½in (1cm) deep
Sandpaper and block
Waterproof PVA glue
Paintbrush
Surgical and rubber gloves
Powder adhesive and additive
Two buckets for mixing
Margin trowel
Notched trowel: ¼in (3mm)
Sponge
Awl or similar tool
Marble sealant and brush
White powder grout and additive
Grout float
Cloth
Galvanized steel table base

MARBLE TESSERAE COLORS

White with gray flecks
Black

USING THE TEMPLATE

Detach the template at the back of the book. In this project, the template is not transferred onto the surface that you plan to mosaic, but is used as a pattern guide that you can follow when laying the tesserae.

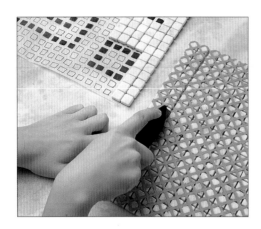

1 Place the marble tesserae onto the template in the correct position. A quick and easy method of doing this is to leave the tesserae on the backing paper, and cut along whole rows with a craft knife.

2 Remove any rough edges from the plywood with sandpaper and a block. Then seal with PVA glue using a brush. Leave until the edges are dry to touch. Wearing rubber gloves, mix some powder adhesive, and apply with a margin trowel.

3 Still wearing rubber gloves, drag a notched trowel toward you across the adhesive, creating a grooved surface on which to place the tesserae. These grooves provide a good tooth to which the mosaic pieces can adhere.

4 Start transferring the tesserae from the template to the board. The backing paper can be left stuck to the tesserae. Stick the tesserae onto the adhesive in rows, using the template as a pattern guide. The tesserae should be stuck face up. Once all tesserae have been positioned, allow to dry for 24 hours.

5 Clean the mosaic with a damp sponge and remove any unwanted adhesive using an awl or similar tool. As the table will be used outside, apply a sealant before grouting. Paint the sealant on with a brush and allow to dry.

6 Wearing rubber gloves, mix up some white powder grout (see page 9) and apply using a float. Push the grout firmly into the gaps and then sponge off any excess using circular movements. Allow the mosaic to dry for another 24 hours.

7 Reapply the marble sealant to the tabletop for protection, and allow to dry completely before you move onto the next step. The sealant will prevent the marble mosaic pieces from becoming discolored by grout or dirt.

8 Slot the completed tabletop into position. Mix a small amount of white grout and apply to the edges of the table using a float. Wipe clean and polish with a dry cloth.

HINTS AND TIPS

▶ Ask your supplier for advice on what type of sealant is best for the tesserae that you are using.

▶ If you plan to commission your own table, then ask the metal artist to allow for a small gap between the wooden top and the metal rim of the table. This will allow the mosaic top to slot into place easily. If you are planning to use a readymade table, then adjust your mosaic template to allow for this.

▶ Wear an apron or smock to protect your clothing from adhesive and grout because stains are almost impossible to remove.

▶ Work in small sections when grouting your mosaic. This will enable you to wipe away any excess before it dries hard.

▶ The abrasive edge of a scouring pad is ideal for removing dry cement from tesserae. However, do not use a green scouring pad because pieces can get stuck and stain the grout. For the same reason, do not use steel wool for this job.

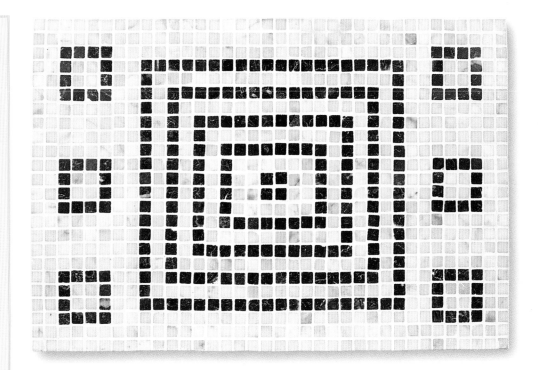

INSPIRATIONAL IDEAS

For a less ambitious project, you could use just the central part of the template to create a mosaic tile.

Alternately, you could enlarge the template and create a stunning mosaic floor.

8036 Enterprise Street
Burnaby, B.C.
V5A 1V7 Canada
Tel (604) 415-2444
Fax (604) 415-3444

ISBN 1-894722-57-4

Commissioning Editor: Natasha Martyn-Johns
Project Editor: Sarah Wilde
Designer: Cathy Layzell
Managing Editor: Anna Osborn
Design Manager: Helen Taylor
Photo Librarian: Bobbie Leah
Photographers: Graeme Ainscough, Lauren Shear
Stylists: Caroline Davis, Nicole Albert

CEO: Robert Oerton
Publisher: Catie Ziller
Production Manager: Lucy Byrne
International Sales Director: Kevin Lagden

Printed and bound in China through The Hanway Press Ltd